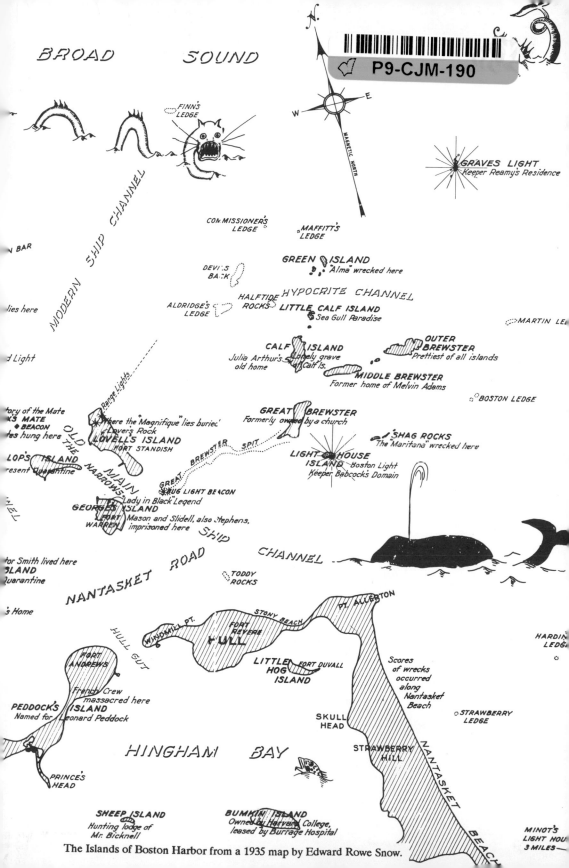

BROAD SOUND

GRAVES LIGHT
Keeper Reamy's Residence

MODERN SHIP CHANNEL

FINN'S LEDGE

COMMISSIONER'S LEDGE

MAFFITT'S LEDGE

N BAR

GREEN ISLAND
"Alma" wrecked here

DEVIL'S BACK

HYPOCRITE CHANNEL

HALFTIDE ROCKS

ALDRIDGE'S LEDGE

LITTLE CALF ISLAND
Sea Gull Paradise

lies here

MARTIN LEE

CALF ISLAND
Julia Arthur's old home

Lonely grave on Calf Is.

OUTER BREWSTER
Prettiest of all islands

d Light

MIDDLE BREWSTER
Former home of Melvin Adams

BOSTON LEDGE

Range Lights

ory of the Mate
K'S MATE
♦ BEACON
tes hung here

"Where the "Magnifique" lies buried"
Lover's Rock
LOVELL'S ISLAND
FORT STANDISH

GREAT BREWSTER
Formerly owned by a church

GREAT BREWSTER SPIT

SHAG ROCKS
The "Maritana" wrecked here

LIGHT HOUSE ISLAND
Boston Light Keeper Babcock's Domain

OLD THE NARROWS

LOP'S ISLAND
resent Quarantine

MAIN

BUG LIGHT BEACON
Lady in Black Legend

GEORGES ISLAND
FORT WARREN
Mason and Slidell, also Stephens, imprisoned here

SHIP

CHANNEL

or Smith lived here
ISLAND
Quarantine

NANTASKET ROAD

TODDY ROCKS

PT. ALLERTON

HARDIN LEDGE

s Home

HULL GUT

WINDMILL PT.

STONY BEACH

FORT REVERE

HULL

FORT ANDREWS

French Crew massacred here

PEDDOCK'S ISLAND
Named for Leonard Peddock

LITTLE HOG ISLAND

FORT DUVALL

Scores of wrecks occurred along Nantasket Beach

STRAWBERRY LEDGE

SKULL HEAD

STRAWBERRY HILL

NANTASKET

HINGHAM BAY

PRINCE'S HEAD

SHEEP ISLAND
Hunting lodge of Mr. Bicknell

BUMKIN ISLAND
Owned by Harvard College, leased by Burrage Hospital

BEACH

MINOT'S LIGHT HOU
3 MILES

The Islands of Boston Harbor from a 1935 map by Edward Rowe Snow.

A LIGHTHOUSE FAMILY

by Harold B. Jennings

The Lovell's Island range lights in Boston Harbor.

Graves Light in Boston Harbor.

Library of Congress Catalog Card Number 89-89575

*Printed in the United States of Americay by
    Bookcrafters, Incorporated, Chelsea, Michigan*

*Published by the Lower Cape Publishing Co.,
    P.O. Box 901, Orleans, Mass. 02653*

FIRST EDITION

ISBN 0-936972-12-2

The Boston Light dates back to 1715. It is the oldest light station in the United States.

INTRODUCTION

In the year 1989, the United States Lighthouse Service will be two hundred years old. The oldest lighthouse in the United States, Boston Light, will be the last lighthouse to go automatic. I have had the thrill of being brought up in the lighthouse service when the lights were still lit by kerosene and we had to row ashore. I have had the honor of being a lighthouse keeper (a wickie) when I was eighteen. This is my youth on Lovell's Island range light in Boston Harbor. You will meet Dad the tease, I was the apple of his eye.

While you read this true story of my life as a lighthouse keepers son, you will be enjoying the adventures I had as a youth on the island. You will get involved with the humor of my Dad and realize the level headedness and discipline of Mom. How I went to school, how we got the seven miles from the island to Boston. You will travel by boat, light a lighthouse and set around the kitchen table after a hearty meal and listen to Dad tell his many sea stories as we adventure in to the past you will know "A Lighthouse Family".

Mom and Dad sitting on the front steps of the Keeper's Quarters on Boston where he was stationed from 1916 to 1919.

DEDICATION

I dedicate these memories to my Mom and Dad who did so much for me over the years. To my wife Hattie who kept after me to "Work on your book, why don't you?" Also to my son and family who know how to make a Dad proud. And to all the lighthouse buffs who help to keep the lights burning.

CONTENTS

CREDITS

Thanks go to Ruth Sanford of New Jersey for many hours word processing from my tapes and to her Mom who was our best critic. Also to John Ullman of Eastham who said the words I was waiting to hear: "You have a book".

Minots Ledge Light in the early days. Note the lifeboat on davits.

Chapter One

The Family History, a change in service, Monomoy Light-1909, and Transferred to Lovell's Island-our home.

My Dad fished on a schooner like this one out of Provincetown harbor.

Cahoon's Hollow Life Saving Station, South Wellfleet (Cape Cod) Mass.

The Cahoon's Hollow Life Saving Station, South Wellfleet, Cape Cod, Mass. My Dad served at this station from 1902 to 1907. *Post Card courtesy of Stanley Snow, Orleans, Mass.*

Chapter One

Dad was born in Provincetown, Massachusetts, at the tip of Cape Cod on August 5, 1878 and departed March 1, 1940. Mom was born in Orrington, Maine, April 3, 1882 and departed February 19, 1972. Mom moved to Provincetown as a small child and she and Dad went through school together. At the time of their marriage, Dad was a fisherman. He wanted a steadier job. He applied for and was appointed to the United States Lifesaving Service in 1902. This job meant he had to walk the back beaches of Cape Cod. He no sooner got in, when he found he had to take his turn cooking and he "couldn't boil water without burning it". Each time he came home on leave, he would learn more about cooking. As time went by, he came to enjoy it and became a great cook. After a few cooking lessons, he volunteered to do all the cooking if the others would take his beach patrol. They agreed as no one else liked to cook. His lifesaving station was Cahoon's Hollow in Wellfleet and his pay was $450 per year.

3

Above: The Cape Ann light station on Thatcher's Island. **Below:** The Monomoy light station on Monomoy Island off Chatham.

After five years in the lifesaving service, Dad applied for a job with the United States Lighthouse Service. At that time the lighthouse service was under the Department of Commerce. In 1939, the service was taken over by the Coast Guard. On February 24, 1907, Dad received his letter of acceptance which read: "You have been accepted for duty on Thatcher's Light off Cape Ann, Gloucester, Massachusetts. How soon can you arrive?" Dad wrote on the back of the letter: "Where do I send my furniture?" He became the fourth assistant Keeper at a salary of $660 per year. At that time, furniture was moved to and from the island on an eighteen foot dory. When Mom and Dad bought an upright piano it had to be tied across two eighteen foot dories. I don't know how it ever stayed tuned. Dad remained on Thatcher's Light for about two years. His next assignment was keeper on the Monomoy Light Station on the Monomoy Islands off Chatham, back on Cape Cod, at a salary of $660 per year. This time a buoy tender moved the furniture.

Each station had a different type of housing. One type of lighthouse has just a tower with no land showing around it. This tower would often be manned by two or three men whose families lived ashore in "station" houses. This same type of tower might house a whole family which would mean that the wife and children would (and did in many cases) have a turn in running the light when the keeper got caught ashore for some reason. Another type of light station is surrounded by land. The house or houses are separate from the tower. This could be located on an island or on the mainland. Monomoy was an island.

On the island Dad and Mom had a cow, chickens and a horse and buggy. At low tide in those days, you could drive a horse and buggy across the flats to Chatham. There is a story my mother used to tell about going to town with the horse. When crossing the wet part of the flats you had to get out of the buggy and lead the horse as there were areas of quicksand and the horse would get mired in it. This particular day, Dad was leading the horse and the reins slipped from his hands. When he reached down for the reins, a ring my mother had given him slipped off his finger. He searched in vain but could not find it. Every time he crossed the flats for the next three years he would look for it. Mom would say, "Charles, you know you can't find that ring, especially with the tide coming in and out across those flats." In the meantime, in May, 1916, Dad applied for and was accepted as keeper of the Boston Light. The day before he was to leave the Monomoy station, he told Mom that he was going to go and find the ring. She told him he was wasting his time.

Above: The assistant keeper's house at Boston Light. **Below:** Mom and the raccoon at Boston Light.

Believe it or not, he went to the area where he had lost the ring a few years earlier and there it was! Some time when we meet, ask me about the other mystery concerning this ring, (especially if you believe in the supernatural).

Dad was appointed Keeper of Boston Light at a salary of $804 per year (later raised to $960 per year). On February 3, 1918 the *USS Alacrity*, a Coast Guard patrol boat,ran aground in the ice a few yards from the station. The tide was ebbing (going out) fast and it wasn't long before the vessel lay over on her side. This made it impossible for the crew to launch their life boat. Dad and the assistant keeper saw their plight and began figuring how to rescue the crew. They reasoned that if they tried to get a dory through the ice cakes, they would be crushed. Dad remembered that in the boat house there was some gun powder and firing caps that were used in the old cannon, originally used as a fog signal at the light. The assistant keeper got a coil of rope that could be used. They set the fuse and pushed the gun powder down the barrel. They made a hard ball in the end of the rope. The remaining coil laid next to the cannon. The fuse was ignited and when the gun fired, the rope followed the ball out to the ship. It was not quite on target so they tried again with no success. Now they had to launch the dory and take a chance that the ice did not close in on them. After a couple of trips, carrying the crew and gear, the rescue was a success. This was the last time the fog cannon was fired at Boston Light.

While on Boston Light, a raccoon appeared on the island. No one knows how he got there. Maybe he was feeding at the beach on the mainland, got on a board and floated out to Little Brewster Island. Mom fed it and tamed it. Dad and the raccoon didn't always get along. The reason being that Dad was a big tease. One day the raccoon was straddling the outside water barrel getting a drink. Dad came up behind him and pushed him in. Boy was he mad. While Dad was keeper of Boston Light, the two hundredth anniversary of that station was celebrated. The (then) Secretary of Commerce officiated at the celebration.

In 1919, Dad became the keeper of the Lovells Island Range Light Station which was about a mile and a half inshore from Boston Light. He was the sole keeper there for twenty years. He now had two lights to care for but he took a cut in salary to $840 per year. I do not know why. Here is where I came into the picture (February 12, 1921) two years after they arrived on Lovells Island.

Above: The Boston Light station in Boston harbor. **Below:** On September 16, 1916, the Secretary of Commerce, William C. Redfield, on the right, is shaking hands with Charles H. Jennings, head lighthouse keeper at Boston Light on the occasion of the two hundredth anniversary celebration of the beacon.

Above: An aerial photograph of the north end of Lovell's Island in Boston harbor showing the range lights and the keepers house on the left. This photograph was made sometime in the 1930's. **Below:** An aerial photograph taken in February, 1989 of the north end of Lovell's Island. This is a different angle than the photo above, showing years of erosion have taken a toll on the property. Just to the right of center is what is left of the foundation of one of the light towers. It is now under water at high tide.

Above: This is my Dad carrying wood from the wood shed before the trestle was connected to it. There is an oil can on the step. This is the oil he carried up into the lights each night at light-up time. **Below Left:** This is the carriage that I hung over the side and grabbed Frenchie the cat's tail. **Below Right:** This is my Dad and I when I was very young.

Lovells Island is an island of approximately seventy three acres and about a quarter of a mile across at its widest point. It is about seven miles from Boston and about one and a half miles from Hull, Massachusetts. This island was basically a fort (Fort Standish). The lighthouse service owned a triangle section on the north end of the island just big enough to put a house, woodshed, two towers and an oil shed. All of the buildings were connected by a seven-foot high trestle and the foundation of the house was seven feet also. The reason was that when there were winter northeasters, the big waves broke over the sea wall and flooded the interior of the island at our end. I loved that because then I could go out in the small rowboat by myself.

Once, when I was about six years old, I got caught in cat-o-nine-tail weeds and started to scream (Mom said I had a bad temper). Dad got worried and, from the trestle, tried to explain how I could get loose. But I just got madder and wouldn't listen until Mom stepped in and yelled "You got yourself into this, now get yourself out." Then the two of them went into the house. I was the apple of my Dad's eye while Mom did the disciplining. So, when she said "get yourself out" that is just what I had to do! Knowing Dad, he was watching through the front door as was my mother. She cared!
I got out.

Behind the house to the north, there was a big (man-made) hill which hid three six inch disappearing guns. In the center of the island was another big hill that hid three ten-inch disappearing guns. On the top of the hill were three, three-inch anti-aircraft guns and at the south end of the island were three, three-inch field guns. I understand they were brought from France after World War I. Also on the south end of the island were houses where three army caretakers and their families lived and other buildings such as barracks, mess halls and stables where the mules were kept.

The lighthouse property contained the main seven room house. A woodshed next to the house stored the wood for the kitchen as well as paints and tools. There were two towers, "range lights" meaning one shown over the other. When a ship was coming up the "Hypocrite Channel", the helmsman held the ship on course with the lights lined up to keep in the channel and not go aground. Between the two towers, there was an oil house where the drums of kerosene were stored. This was the fuel for the lights. Later, a five-hundred gallon tank was installed on the bank near the house. Connecting the house, the woodshed, the oil house and the two light towers was a trestle, seven feet above the ground. It was just wide enough for two people to walk side by side, but it was tight.

Everything was made of wood and this material required paint. Painting was going on most of the time and maybe that is why I don't like to paint today. On a lighthouse, the whole family chips in with the work. After I painted the stairs to the oil house, I could go and play. That little chore used to seem like punishment. The tops of both towers were made of steel where the lantern rooms were. The insides of the towers also had to be painted and vanished. I can remember Dad connecting (by ropes) a sixteen foot ladder to the top of a thirty-two foot extension ladder. He hoisted it

The light keeper's house on Lovell's Island. The hill to the left of the house hides the disappearing guns. At a young tender age I posed for the photograph.

12

Above: At our home on Lovell's Island, Mom and Dad posed on the front porch. **Below:** This photograph was taken as the boat approached the Army dock. The Lovell's Island range lights are in the background.

up the side of the tower or house and painted from there. Its a wonder he didn't get killed.

Inside the triangle and near the house, Dad had a garden every year. We also had chickens, ducks and turkeys throughout my youth. I don't know why we never had cattle because it would have been an ideal place for them. Dad had a soft heart towards animals and I guess it would have been hard for him to have them prepared for the table.

At about five years of age, I found a friend to play with. His Dad was one of the Army caretakers on the island. Although there was no electricity on the island, we had a telephone. Mom would call my friend's mother and say, "Send Buster on his way, I'll watch for him." Between our house and the Army family houses on the other end of the island was a hill and a curve so you couldn't see the other homes. Mom would let me go to meet Buster when he came to play with me and when I went to his house, the call was reversed and Buster came to meet me. Whey the concern of our mothers? The dirt road ran from behind our house to the far end of the island. On the inland side of the road were high hills with only a few feet to the water on the water-side of the road. You know how children are tempted to roam where they shouldn't.

****

Thats "Buster" Hamil on the left and me on the right. We are standing about half way between his house and ours.

14

Chapter Two

Transportation to and from the island, and my early school days.

Left: A photograph of my Dad on the Army dock wearing his Lightkeepers hat.
Right: A photograph of my Mom.

The army boat L-52, approaching the dock.

Chapter Two:

How did we get back and forth from the island to the mainland? Of course, it was by boat. On this island there was a fort, served by army boats which were fifty to one hundred feet long. Up until the 1930's, we traveled on the larger boats which were steamers. They burned coal that made the steam to run the engines. The three I remember were the *Bachelder, Jessup,* and the *General Anderson.* They came out of the army base in South Boston and delivered the mail, food and other cargo for the soldiers and their families. In the early 1930's, there were six army-occupied islands (Forts Strong, Standish, Warren, Andrews, Duvall and Revere). As the military was cut back, there were only three or four families on each island as caretakers. The boats I have the fondest memories of were the L-52, and the L-48. These boats were fifty-two feet long, one mast, clear deck forward, a pilot house behind the mast, a low profile deck house over the engine room and aft of the engine room, a small compartment with a pot belly coal burning stove with a row of seats on each side that would seat eight or ten people. There was a small deck aft. This boat was used to work the sunken harbor mines that were set during World War I. During the month of July, the army

Grammy Rogers, the "Devil"

would have mine practice.

On one of our trips from the mainland, after school, we were on the L- 52. The wind was blowing out of the northwest a good thirty to forty miles per hour. This made docking a bit wild. The tide was low - fifteen feet from the boat to the top of the dock. I looked up at the ladder they rigged from the boat to the dock and I got scared. Dad and two other men were on the dock and the boat crew were next to me. Dad told me to watch and time the waves. When the boat started to rise, I was to start up the ladder fast. I got half way up when the boat decided to go down. Dad hollered at me to lie flat and hang on. The moment I laid flat, the three men on the pier pulled me and the ladder up on to the dock. Scared, you bet!

During the course of my school years I often traveled on the Boston police boats and one year we traveled on the Boston fireboats. There were times when we traveled on the quarantine boat from Gallops Island. After Dad was assigned an eighteen-foot Swampscott dory by the lighthouse service, we rowed to the mainland.

You are probably thinking that when you live on an island you don't have to go to school. I had to go to school. The U.S. Government paid the different towns to allow us to go to their schools. My first year was at Hull Village School. There was a lighthouse just a few yards to the south of our island called the "Narrows Light" (better known as "Bug Light"). The lighthouse keeper and his wife (Mr. and Mrs. Tom Small) had a son (Jimmy) who was my age so the two mothers agreed to rent a house in the village and share the expenses. The mothers took turns staying with us and on Friday night we would take the army boat home to our island and then Jimmy's father would row over to pick him up. Sunday (if the weather was good) one or the other of our fathers would row us to Hull. If the weather was bad, we waited until Monday morning and took the Army boat to Hull. This made us about an hour late for school.

My second year of school was at a school in South Boston. Here my mother ran a small candy and variety store on Ward Street. My third year was at East Boston. I remember this school for two reasons. The bridge across Chelsea Creek turned half way across to let boats through and when we kids heard a boat whistle for it to open, we ran down so we could ride on it. The second reason was the Chinese twins in my class. The first twins I had ever seen. My fourth grade was in Salem. Why so far from Boston where the boats left to go to the island? Well, my Uncle Lew (Llewellyn Rogers) was

Above Left: Miss Bailey was my teacher on the Island. She was a good teacher but I could hear my Dad working about and I was distracted from my studies, so that was the last year for a tutor. **Above Right:** My cousin Delmont with "Henny Penny" on his shoulder. I am on the right. This was the chicken I used to play with - I used to dress her up and try to feed her when she really didn't want to be fed. She would never try to run away though. **Below:** The Norwood family that I boarded with for two years. I have fond memories of Faye, Bruce, Wanda, Priscilla, Dexter, Ralph, Georgia and two other boys. Mr. & Mrs. Norwood are on the right in the back row.

keeper of the Graves Light at the northeast entrance to Boston Harbor and his home station was at Salem Willows at the Old Pickering Light property. My aunt had died so my grandmother Rogers was taking care of my cousin Delmont. This made it nice for me and my parents. We used to ride the streetcars from Salem Willows to school.

My grandmother was a small petite old fashioned lady, but she was a devil. After a big snow storm, Delmont (two years older than I) suggested that we pretend to be sick and after the streetcar had gone, we could feel better and then be able to go out and play in the snow. I looked up to Delmont as I would a big brother so I went along with him. We moaned and groaned so my grandmother came up to find out what the trouble was. Grammy Rogers had a cure for all sickness and if the doctors used it today, their offices would only be open one day a week. This medicine was called "Tincture of Rhubarb" and looked and tasted like an iodine and mercurochrome mix. Grammy said, "You boys lie in bed and rest and I will be right back." (We should have known.) Soon, up the stairs came Grammy with a spoon and that wicked bottle. Without her even unscrewing the cap of the bottle, we became well and able to go to school. That year I traveled to school on the Boston police boat out of Station eight on Atlantic Avenue, Boston. That same year, we also traveled some of the time on the Boston fireboats as the new police boat did not handle correctly and was not accepted by the City of Boston.

For my fifth and sixth grades in school, I had a private tutor furnished by the state of Massachusetts. (I still have the desk that Santa brought by tow boat for me to use during this period.) This wasn't good because I missed having someone else to play with and I was alone a lot of the time. Also, I could hear my dad working about and this was distracting. My seventh and eighth grades were back in Hull. Three years of high school were at Hingham High (Hull students at that time went to Hingham by bus). I stayed with two different families during that time. They were memorable times because both families were large. I stayed with the Norwood family from Boston Light for my seventh and eighth grades, and then the Van Scoyoc Family on the army post in Hull (Fort Revere) for the next three years of school. While in Hull, I traveled on the army boats (the L boats). Fort Revere in Hull was the boat's last stop before it started back to Winthrop (Fort Banks). In the winters when the harbor froze over we didn't get home on some weekends. We never seemed to miss any school, I guess our parents made sure of that.

During the winter of 1929-30, I scraped up some snow, packed it in a box to make cakes. I carted it in my wagon and made an igloo. It was tough work as most of the snow had melted.

Chapter Three

Christmas time, rowing to get there, driftwood fuel
and Mother's discipline.

Above: Captain Wincapaw was the first flying Santa in 1928. The flights were sponsored by the La Touraine Coffee Company. The plane was a Bellanca Airbus. **Below:** The flying Santa in the 1970's, Edward Rowe Snow, dropped a package for me at Nauset Light house in Eastham.

Chapter Three:

On the island were soft (white) pine trees and it was a great event to trudge through the snow and pick out a Christmas tree. Home it would come and on Christmas Eve we decorated. I had to go to bed early on that night as I couldn't be up when Santa Claus came (by towboat). The towboat captains all knew Dad and when passing they would blow a salute of three blasts on their whistles and I never knew on which towboat Santa would arrive. We had no electricity but everything was beautifully decorated. Dad would make a toy for me every Christmas. I still have a lighthouse and a four stack destroyer. He made me a barge one year which had thread spools for drums to coil ropes and the derricks went up and down - a joy.

In 1928, when I was seven years old, Captain Bill Wincapaw started the Flying Santa. It was sponsored by the La Touranie Coffee company. The plane flew along the New England coast parachuting gifts to personnel in the lighthouses and lightships along the way. Captain Wincapaw was the pilot. He flew until 1939 and then went to Chile to fly machines over the Andes where he was lost in a crash. Following him, the flying Santa was taken over by Edward Rowe Snow, the historian who wrote many books about the New England area and flew until his death in 1983. As a lad, it was great to see Santa leaning out the plane door in his red suit waving a Christmas greeting, and then run after the parachuted package which would contain pencils, paper, coloring and story books, candy, gifts for the ladies and cigarettes for Dad.

The plane then flew over the lightships with a long rope dragging and aimed to hit the cable that goes from the top of the mast to the bow - letting it spin around the "forward stay" until the package would slide down to the deck. Incidentally, the last gift I received from the flying Santa (when I was in my fifties) was a book written by Edward Rowe Snow. He found out that I lived in North Eastham on Cape Cod and flew over just before Christmas that year and dropped it at Nauset Light for me. Santa in his red suit was still waving from that plane. I read recently that the flying Santa tradition continues to this day - flown by an individual living in Hull.

25

Also around Christmas time, an army boat would come at night and take the island kids and their parents up to a Christmas party at Fort Banks in Winthrop so we could see Santa. The night crews of these army boats were not as knowledgeable about the harbor as the day crews. One night, coming out of Winthrop through a narrow, muddy channel, another boy and I were standing between the wheel and the forward windows of the pilot house and it didn't look to us as though the fellow steering the boat was in the channel. In those days you were supposed to be seen and not heard, and NEVER told an adult what to do. But it bothered me so much, I turned to my mother, who was sitting on a bench behind the wheel, and said, "Mom, we're out of the channel and going to run aground." She said, "Son, mind your own business; the gentleman knows what he is doing." A few minutes later we slid into the mud. We lay there from 9:00 p.m. until 3:00 a.m. when the tide came back in. A pot-bellied stove was the only heat we had to ward off the bitter cold and wind which blew across an area that was later filled to become Logan Airport in Boston.

In the summer, our transportation was an eighteen-foot bank dory with two sets of oars plus a steering oar. The town of Hull was the nearest point and we would go there or to Gallops Island and take the quarantine boat to Boston. The direction we took to go to Hull depended upon which way the tide was going. If it was coming in you would go east of George's Island and if the tide was going out you would go west of George's Island (Fort Warren). After going through Hull Gut, if the tide was running out, we stayed to the west towards Paddocks Island (Fort Andrews) and shot across the channel on an angle and got in that way. If the tide was coming in we went out to the east towards Boston light then rushed in with the tide, went through the narrows and turned into the pier.

Dad would seat the passengers and when doing so would have to use a little diplomacy to keep the boat balanced (especially when seating the ladies). He would look the ladies over to judge their weights and say "I think we had better have so and so sit there and you sit here." If one of the ladies would say, "Well, I want to sit there," he would answer "Never mind - you have to sit here." He couldn't tell them the weight had to be aft in the dory - and say "You're heavier than the other ladies" and so he used a little discretion and said "in an eighteen-foot dory, this is the best seat."

When we got onto the shore back at the island, we had to beach the boat and get all of the passengers out. Then we had to roll the boat out of the water because the tides and winds were often fierce. You would have four planks, each about twelve feet long, plus two rollers about five to six inches in diameter and about four feet long. Lay one roller across the planks and then put the bow on the roller across the planks and everybody would push - ladies and all. Then the next roller was laid under the bow on the other two planks and you would run like the devil back to the stern - one on each side of the dory - and grab the two planks you just came off of and run those planks up to the bow. It would probably take five times that you had to relay these planks and rollers to get the boat from the low water mark on to the beach and the safety of the sands. High tide was much better. Sometimes we anchored the dory in good weather and waited for high tide so you wouldn't have to roll it quite so far. Of course, the fun for us kids was grabbing the boards and dragging them up and running like the devil and trying to get them up there before the dory got all the up onto the next roller. If it once fell off the boards you would get stuck in the sand and have to lift it and put the boat back on the roller. The whole operation would be reversed to launch the dory.

The lighthouse service never furnished us a power boat because we had transportation by the army, fire, and police boats, but they managed to supply us with their oldest dories. My dad used to say that when the service did not want a dory any longer, they gave it to him. When I was about five years old, we had a power dory called the Apache. It had an old make and break engine in it. When you turned the fly wheel over if she kicked the right way, she would go ahead; if she didn't kick the right way, the engine would be going the wrong way and you would have to shut her off and kick her again. The Apache had a big spray hood and we used to get under it and she would cruise right along. Later on, we did acquire an outboard. I'll tell you later on what happened to that.

After landing on the island from the mainland, as you came over the edge of the sand dunes, you could see the two towers, the oil house and the main house where we lived. We usually had a big army push cart to take groceries, etc. to the house. Every time you came back from the beach you had to bring in an armload of driftwood because we burned coal and wood. It was my job to fill the woodshed with wood for the winter. It took quite a bit. We would go down to the beach and pick bushels and bushels of wood. It was quite a chore to get the wood in for the winter. Mom baked every Friday and she had to have three bushels of wood to do the cooking.

Above: The old power boat APACHE, with the "make and break" engine. **Below:** My dog "Betsy" and I near the stairs leading to the house. In the background is the Hudson automobile.

One day when I was in a hurry to get to my boat, I put some rocks in the bushel baskets and covered them with wood. I lugged them up eleven plus four steps to get to the house and asked my mother if I could then go out on the boat. I had the most miserable day because I knew what the results of my action were going to be because my mother didn't have enough wood to do the baking. I came back expecting to be restricted or punished. When I got back, there were cakes and pies all over and supper was ready. Nothing was said. During supper, I couldn't stand it any longer and I said, "Mom, did you have enough wood today?" She said, "Son, if I had you five minutes after you left I would have warmed your bottom, but after a while it became funny to me, but this is the last time it is going to be funny." It was the last time.

You have to realize, I was Dad's pride and joy. If he had his way, I would have been spoiled rotten. Mom did the disciplining. Oh yes, I got a spanking now and then. I deserved them. I remember one time I had done something wrong. I can't remember what it was but it must have involved Dad because Mom made Dad take me upstairs to give me a spanking and put me to bed. Dad began making excuses for me but Mom insisted. Upstairs, we went into my bedroom. Then dad said: "Son you yell and then get into bed." Well Mom did not like the tone of my yelling and came upstairs, opened the door and there was Dad laying in the bed with me and hugging me. "Well," Mom said, "Charles, you spank that child or I will." So Dad spanked me. Remember, Mom was not cruel. She had a heart of gold and a hand of steel.

One other time, I did something wrong but this time I was older and in the back entry Mom had a small branch from a tree and if I needed some discipline, I got the backs of my legs tapped. I figured it out that if I throw that switch out, I won't get spanked. So I did. Soon after, I did something wrong. Mom went to get the switch and of course it was gone. She said, "Son, you go out and find another switch of the same size. If you can't find one I will." Then I knew I better do this properly. Have you ever gone out to choose a switch that is to be used on yourself?

Above: I must have been four or five years old when this picture was taken. We used to play under the porch. Mom was standing where she killed the eagle after it got caught between the rails of the trestle. The window to the left of the porch was the living room. Above the porch was the master bedroom. Dad could look out the window in the bedroom and see the small windows in the towers. He could tell if the flames in the lamps were burning clean or not. Dad and Grampa Rogers are carrying the ladder. **Below:** This house was on the Army base dock. This was where one waited for the mail boat in bad weather. I am standing so as to cover the SMO in SMOKING.

Chapter Four

Lighting the towers, sunset arriving, I dare you! After sunset and like father, like son.

Dad standing by one of the range lights.

Chapter Four:

There was no electricity. So, how did the lighthouses work? On the northeast side of the lighthouse there was a five foot square window of heavy plate glass. Inside the big tower (the taller one) there was a concaved disc about three feet in diameter similar to those you see on cable television installations today. It was made of nickel and plated with silver and was brightly polished. On the back of the disc was a slot where a lamp protruded up through and it had a wick in it and burned kerosene. This shown out through the window and gave about fifteen miles of light. At the little tower they still had the old prisms that you see in pictures of the insides of most lighthouses. A kerosene lamp inside the lenses gave the light. The light was lit about a half hour before sunset and was blown out a half hour after sunrise. Kerosene table lamps were used in the house. A five-hundred gallon tank of kerosene which lasted a whole year was mounted down near the beach and we had two and five gallon cans to bring oil to the house. There was a black iron stove which is still popular today. It burned wood and coal and was our kitchen heat as well as our cook stove.

When it started to get dark at night, we would beg Dad to take us up to light the tower. "If you can keep your fingers off the brasswork" would be his response. You would take a gallon can of oil with you, proceed along the trestle which ran from the house to the oil shed, from the oil shed to the big tower, and then into the little tower. As we approached the big tower we were reminded again to "keep your fingers off the brasswork". As we entered the tower door, Dad would take the key off the nail (hidden behind the door casing), unlock the bottom door and we would start up the wooden spiral stairs. The stairs were varnished treads with white risers attached to them. As we went up the stairs my Dad would say, "Don't you dare kick the toes of your shoes against the risers". This was not only an instruction but a threat against your life if you should ever mar the paint. Also we heard, "Keep your fingers off the paint work and don't touch any of the brasswork - I have to polish it". There were about fourteen steps to the first landing, six steps to the second landing and about a six or eight foot ladder which led to the lantern room. As you looked up you could see a trap door over your head which was closed. Dad would go up the ladder and push the hatch up with his head. (Maybe that is why he was so bald.)

In the lantern room, we were again reminded to keep our hands off the brasswork and the paint. The lamp was covered with a cloth bag. This was to keep the dust and sun off the reflectors. The lantern room had six sides; on the side towards the smaller tower was a large window of very thick glass. The glass was thick because during the night the light would attract birds such as ducks who flew right into it and the glass had to be thick enough to withstand the impact. The poor birds got killed from the blow. Not too many birds hit the glass, though. On the opposite wall, there was a small, square door which led out onto the deck that circled the tower where the lantern room was attached to the main part of the tower. This catwalk had an iron rail all the way around. We would yell down to mother and if it was not too windy she might hear us. Back in the tower we would take a small brass reservoir tank on the back of the lamp and carefully pour the kerosene into it and then quickly flip the tank upside down into its holder. This would let the oil drip slowly in as needed. It fed the wick of the lamp. This one tank would take the lamp through the night and would burn without going out. The wick was lit with a safety match. Dad would put his finger in the flame to level the wick so it would burn evenly. Then, down the ladder we would go and on to the other tower. "Keep your hands off the woodwork - don't touch the brass". The small tower was lighted the same was as the big tower.

I always wanted to put my finger through that flame as I watched my father level the wick. It took me quite awhile to learn how you could put your finger in a flame of a lamp and not get burned. You would have to bring the wick down to the lowest point and rub your finger all the way around to smooth the burned stuff off so that the wick would burn nice and even and not have smoky ends. After I accomplished this performance, I became brave. It was a big event when I brought someone home as a guest and showed him how I could trim the wick. "Why don't you try it?" I would ask. The poor lad who didn't know how, was scared to put his finger in the flame and I would never tell him how long it took me to get the courage to do it. The wick trimming had to be done every night about nine or ten o'clock on both towers. The lamps were lit at sunset and had to go through the night until sunrise when they were turned off and the lenses covered.

Heading back to the house, it would be getting dark and we might go down to the seawall and watch the sun go down over Boston. As we sat on the seawall, the Custom House, the United Shoe building and a few of the other buildings could be seen one by one as the city lights came on. After such a busy day, we would be tired but we couldn't go to sleep yet. The folks might be sitting in the parlor. The only times it was used was to play the piano, phonograph or sit with guests. We kids could come in but had to sit on the floor very quietly and just listen while we waited for the next step in taking care of the lighthouse. That was 9:00 p.m. when we had to go back into the tower again and make the last trip for the night. Dad would light the hand kerosene lantern on the kitchen table as we got in line and away we'd go - down the catwalk (trestle) to the tower and up the spiral stairs. It was spooky as shadows bounced off the walls of the round tower. Up into the lantern room again, we watched Dad go through the same procedure as before - lifting the chimney, putting his finger in the flame and trimming it and setting it for the night. Down the stairs again, on to the other tower, and finally back again along the catwalk, into the house and to bed.

When I was about five years old, Dad used to light a kerosene lantern to go to the towers or go down to the pier when boats used to come in at night. Once, in the winter, I remember being all bundled up and walking along with him and swinging a little kerosene lantern about eight inches tall which was a miniature of Dad's lantern. I was so proud of my lantern - I can still see it flickering in the dark and I can still smell the kerosene. I trimmed its wick and, when we got back home, I had to clean it with a sheet of crumpled newspaper just like he cleaned his lantern.

35

BRASSWORK

or

THE LIGHTHOUSE KEEPER'S LAMENT

Oh what is the bane of a lightkeeper's life
That causes him worry, struggle and strife,
That makes him use cuss words, and beat at his wife?
       Its Brasswork.

What makes him look ghastly consumptive and thin,
What robs him of health, of vigor and vim,
And cause despair and drives him to sin?
       Its Brasswork.

The devil himself could never invent,
A material causing more world-wide lament
And in Uncle Sam's service about ninety per cent,
       Is Brasswork.

The lamp in the tower, reflector and shade,
The tools and accessories pass in parade
As a matter of fact the whole outfit is made
       Of Brasswork.

The oil containers I polish until,
My poor back is broken, aching; and still
Each gallon and quart, each pint and each gill
       Is Brasswork.

I lay down to slumber all weary and sore,
I walk in my sleep, I awake with a snore
And I'm shining the knob on by bedchamber door.
       That's Brasswork.

From pillar to post, rags and polish I tote
I'm never without them, for you will please note
That even the buttons I wear on my coat
       Are Brasswork.

The machinery clockwork, and fog-signal bell
The coal hods, the dustpans, the pump in the well
Now I'll leave it to you mates, if this isn't - well
                    Brasswork.

I dig, scrub and polish, and work with a might,
And just when I get it all shining and bright,
In comes the fog like a thief in the night:
                    Good-by Brasswork.

I start the next day and when noontime draws near,
A boatload of Summer visitors appear,
For no other purpose, than to smooch and besmear
                    My Brasswork.

So it goes all the Summer, and along in the Fall
Comes the district machinist to overhaul
And rub dirty and greasy paws over all
                    My Brasswork.

And again in the Spring, if perchance it may be,
an efficiency star is awarded to me.
I open the package and what do I see?
                    More Brasswork.

Oh, why should the spirit of mortal be proud,
In the short span of life that he is allowed
If all the lining in every dark cloud
                    Is Brasswork.

And when I have polished until I am cold
And I'm taken aloft to the Heavenly fold
Will my harp and my crown be made of pure gold?
                    No, Brasswork.

By the Man off watch.

The *Alacrity* aground at Boston Light. (Story on page 7)

From: The Boston Post, October 4, 1936

THREE TOOTS FOR THE CAPTAIN

Captain Charles L. Jennings who looks out to sea from Lovell's Island surprised Captain Joseph Kemp, of the Provincetown Boat:

"Why," said Captain Kemp, "If I'd known that's where you live I'd have given you a salute."

The Provincetown boat passes there every day.

Its astonishing how that little three-toots ceremony got around. The captains of the Nantasket and New York boats followed suit. And no wonder. For Captain Jennings added heroic prestige to American seamanship. He was the keeper of Boston Light and was responsible for the saving of the crew of the *Alacrity* in January of 1918. His job was so outstanding that he got a letter of commendation at the time from the U.S. Secretary of the Navy.
P.S. - Lovell's Island is in Boston harbor between Deer Island and George's Island.

Chapter Five

Sunrise duties, a salute from the ship, Dad's story times. Dogs fighting, Sunday events and will it sail?

These gun photographs were taken at Fort Pickens in the Gulf Shores National Park at Pensacola, Florida, in 1987. They are identical to the ones that used to be on Lovell's Island. These are up in the firing position.

Chapter Five:

In the morning, we would hear the rattling of the kitchen stove downstairs as dad got the fire going and shook the ashes down. We would begin to smell coffee and pancakes. You could not stay in bed. "Good morning everybody" and we all sat down. Visiting older folks might ask Dad, "How can you sleep in this lighthouse? All we heard was that bell buoy in the channel going 'gong, gong' all night long." We wouldn't hear it. We got used to it like a ticking clock. The first night for adults was really hard because they couldn't get used to the bell buoy and maybe a tow boat blowing to pass another boat or a freighter going by. It wasn't like the streetcar or traffic running by your house in the city. It was different, but we kids slept.

"What's up for the day?" The first thing we would take off and walk the beach. We would play around the seawalls - scampering over the rocks and racing up and down the beach trying not to get wet. We returned about 10:00 a.m., hungry again and there would be peanut butter and jelly sandwiches and punch. Once in a while, a freighter would go by and we would run down the beach to yell and wave. We would go for a swim about one or two in the afternoon. The tide had to be coming in as the water was cold and the hot sands would warm the water a bit. I learned to swim because I couldn't go out in a boat by myself until I could swim. As it didn't take long to turn blue from the cold, I learned to swim fast. The older folks would sit under umbrellas on the beach in long, old-fashioned swim suits.

Early in the morning, about 8:30, a mail boat came. We had to go down and get the mail, daily paper (Boston Globe) and the milk carrier (containing six quarts of milk and a cake of ice) and carry it all back to the house. Coming off the beach, we would go to the gun placements. We played around these cement-formed gun placements, going underground or up the ladders and to climb on the guns. The guns were huge and when they were fired they recoiled up in the air, fired over the top of the bank, and came down and disappeared. They were called "disappearing" guns. The shell was six inches in diameter.

41

The Provincetown boat *Dorothy Bradford* with a full load of passengers. *Photo by R. Loren Graham, courtesy of the Steamship Historical Society collection at the University of Baltimore Library.*

After supper, we went down to the wharf at 7:00 p.m. to watch the Provincetown boat come into Boston. Over the years it was the *Dorothy Bradford.* We would yell to the passengers who were about five hundred feet from us. The echo would come back as the crowd of people would wave and yell to us. It was quite a thrill. I always carried a police whistle with me and my dad carried one too so that we could keep track of each other. This whistle was used only in case of emergency or to salute another vessel. A salute consisted of three blasts. I would blow my police whistle three times and we would wait a few seconds and all of a sudden the whistle from the steam vessel would finally blow back. The captain had heard our whistle and was answering us back with three blasts. You would answer the three blasts with one whistle as acknowledgment and the captain would do the same thing. This was a friendly hello between boats. It was quite a thrill to run down and get this call back. Mom's ringing of the chow bell would signal that it was time to go home. "Watch out for boards with nails in them and don't run on the seaweed because there might be a board underneath. Stay on the sand."

A Saturday night tradition was beans, frankfurters, homemade bread, and apple pie. All of which smelled delicious. Dad's favorite saying was "eat hearty and give the ship a good name." You did not leave the table after supper. The older folks told their tales and swapped yarns and talked at this time. Youth listened. Dad would say, "Did I ever tell you about the time I was in the lifesaving station at Wellfleet on Cape Cod? - Cahoon's Hollow?" and the stories would start from there. "When I was in the lifesaving service on Cape Cod....." and he would start the story about Cahoon's Hollow. "We had to walk the beach at night to watch for vessels that might be sailing too close to shore and warn them to keep away. During the day someone had gone into town for the mail. News was that a local farmer's bull had gotten loose and it was asked that the lifesaving crew walking the beach watch out for this bull. He was kind of a playful bull.

Walking that night on my watch - it was dark and only the stars were out - there was a little breeze and, listening to the surf on the beach, I was walking in a thoughtful trance. When, all of a sudden, out of the darkness, over the sand dunes, came this galloping object right straight for me. I couldn't outrun this bull, so I ran towards the surf, running as fast as I could, lantern in hand. Just as I got to the edge of the surf the bull got me - right behind the back of the legs. Down I went just like a football player tackled me. My face was within inches of the surf's waves. I got my lantern upright - it hadn't gone out. I didn't know what to do. Finally I turned around and heard this thing swishing like a top that was running down. It stopped. There beside me lay a large fish barrel. The wind had caught it just right and it had started rolling down the beach and I thought it was the bull. Of course, you couldn't go back to the station and tell anyone or you would never outlive it and maybe get a name like 'barrelhead' or 'the bull.' They finally found the bull near Mayo's beach in Wellfleet on the other side of the cape". Stories like this were told at the dinner table from time to time. They were true stories, too. When you saw a twinkle in his eye, my mother and I were aware that the story coming up could be a bit far-fetched. Most were true stories though.

Often, in the early morning, we would hear "dog fights". The dogs were actually seals on the rocks out back of our house. They were big seals and one old one was grey - almost white. He was king of the pack. As the tide went down, they would get up on a rock and fight to keep it and bark at each other. Sometimes we would take a rifle and fire it out the window to shut them up. The big grey seal would always win because he was the oldest. They would really put up a fight for a rock. When we went out on the seawall, we would whistle at them and they would swim quite close to us as they were

43

curious. We never did get one for a pet although over on one of the other islands someone had found a baby seal stranded on the beach and he did stay in a tub of water for a while but he finally got restless and jumped off the wharf and took off to the harbor.

Sunday morning breakfasts might be warmed over beans. In addition, we would probably have bacon and fresh eggs from our chickens, french fried potatoes, toast, jellies, homemade apple pie and homemade cheese. There was homemade grape jelly from wild grapes on the island. All the vegetables that we ate were from our own garden. The birds would chirp, the gulls cry and the seals bark. Ready for a days activity, we would run the stone walls, climb the rocks and go swimming. Sunday morning, small boats by the dozens came out of Boston and the surrounding yacht clubs like Hull and Houghsneck, to fish or picnic on the islands.

Whole families would land on the beach and we would play with the kids. Kids were envious of us - they would have liked to live on an island. Families might leave their Sunday papers or else we would row over to Hull to get a paper. This I looked forward to because ice cream was an extra treat. Conditions would have to be good before we could row and we were supervised with a three foot spyglass. Dad always kept a watchful eye when we kids went out in a boat. We played Indians and in kid fashion tried to keep the people off the island. We picked up colored stones and made treasure chests for them and buried them in different places on the island. In fact, I always thought I should go back and dig. I had a particular place where I buried a can of different stones - with a little note in it. This would have been about fifty-five years ago.

One of our activities was rigging up the lighthouse dory as a sailboat. It took all the line we could find and some old hunks of canvas. The dory did not have a centerboard in it and so we had to take the oars and hang them over the side - the blades set according to the depth and wind - to form a "leeboard". It took two or three of us kids to handle it - you could never do it alone. It never sailed right and we used to work hard to get that thing to sail. We could have rowed it to Hades and back again for the amount of energy it would take to make a sail but it was fun.

Chapter Six

No more rowing, maybe. The summer is over. A lighthouse burns and Buried treasure.

"Bug Light" (so called) was a lighthouse on stilts. It was situated at the end of Great Brewster Spit, south of Lovell's Island.

Chapter Six:

While going to school in Hull, I knew a young lad who came from a family who had money, so they had an outboard. Back in those days, if you had an outboard you were classified as being "well off". It was a small outboard. He lost it overboard and we saw where it went. We told him that we would salvage the outboard for him. He said, "If you find the darn thing you can keep it for the summer". Two of us kids got into a skiff and rowed out to where it was. We took the anchor, grappled it and hooked into the outboard. We hauled it up and took it home. Dad said to take the condenser out of it, put it in the oven and bake it to see if it would go. It baked and we put it all back together. This was my first outboard and, wow, I was working on an engine. We put it in a fish barrel and filled the barrel with water after we got it back together. We kept trying to get it going. Dad and a friend helped and all of a sudden it started up. But when it started up we couldn't shut it off and the barrel started coming apart. The water began squirting out through the seams of the barrel staves and finally, when the barrel was about ready to collapse, someone reached over and pulled the wire right off the spark plug. It stopped. But, the motor ran!

Now we had Dad's permission to use the outboard on the dory. The dory was an eighteen-foot fishing dory and it was very high out of water. This motor was not designed with a long shaft and did not even reach the water. How were we going to get this thing to hang on the back of the dory and reach the water? We stuck it on the back of the dory and went down the beach where there was some nice round rocks the size of grapefruits. We loaded them into the back of the boat. We finally got the dory down where the outboard would reach the water. But the bow was way up in the air and you couldn't walk up in the bow because the motor would come out of the water.

In the meantime, my aunt in Wellfleet on Cape Cod became sick. My Mother wanted to go and take care of her and asked us to take her to Hull. That was where we kept our family car. This was great. We could use the outboard. The motor took us all the way over there - about one and a half miles. Here we were, motoring with an outboard. We came around the "Hull Gut", through the tide rips and came up to the float at the pier. We decided to run the bow right up on the float. It went up on the float and down came the bow. We were on top of the float. We shut the motor off and Mom got out and she went on her way. We tried to get off the float but the dory was too heavy and we had to get help. Then, we went back home.

About a week later, when it was time for Mom to come back, we motored over proudly to pick her up. This time we didn't put the bow up on the float because we had to have help getting it off the float the last time. On the way home, halfway between Georges Island (Fort Warren) and the mainland, the motor stalled. Delmont (my cousin) and I tried and tried to get it started but it was getting hot in the sun and my mother said: "you boys pick up those oars and start rowing". Begrudgingly, we rowed back to the island. We had more trouble with that motor. We were coming into the pier one day and it wouldn't shut off. We went right up underneath the pier and almost wrecked the dory. That was it. Dad demanded, "Take that motor back". We rowed over to Hull and gave it back to the fellow who lost it. That was the end of the big adventure with an outboard. All told, we probably had it about four weeks and then it was back to the oars.

Summer was over and, it was back to school. It was one and a half miles (by water) when school was in Hull. The first day of school the army boat took us over on Sunday to get our clothing and gear over. On Friday, we would meet the boat down at the pier in Hull about 4:00 p.m. to go home. On Monday morning the boat would pick us up at 8:00 a.m. and we would be in Hull by 8:30. We were usually an hour late for school but they allowed for us to be late. When I got to high school, the police boat took us over on Sunday night so we could catch an early Monday morning school bus for the twelve mile trip to Hingham High School.

The army boat crew consisted of an engineer, captain and deck hand - all army personnel. As we kids had handled lines all of our lives they would let us throw the heaving line (a small line attached to the larger line) up to the pier. People on the pier hauled in the bigger line which was about two inches in diameter and drop it over a big iron post called a bit. On one of the islands where we used to stop (Georges Island - Fort Warren) there was a lady who always got in front of the bits and thus got in the way. This heaving line had a "monkey fist" on the end of it - a round ball made of rope. In those days they would put a little hunk of lead as big around as a golf ball inside this rope to give it weight. They used to tell us to stay clear so we wouldn't get hit by the fist.

48

We were coming into Fort Warren and it was my turn to throw the heaving line. One of the army fellows said, "I bet you a dime you can't hit her" (the lady who always stood in front of the bit). I of course would never want to hit her. I threw the heaving line and it went over one of her shoulders and when it bit up, it snapped around, came under the other armpit, curved right up and hit her under her chin. Its a wonder it didn't break her teeth but it didn't. Well, I was scared. I didn't realize she should not have been there in the first place. The fellow walked over and handed me a dime. After that, she never stood in front of the bits.

We enjoyed steering the boats as well. I remember we used to go up to Boston on the big army steamers which were one hundred or so feet long - a regular steamboat. Dad and the captain would sit up on the couch behind the steering wheel and I would be up on a high stool and this great big wheel was about five feet in diameter. I would climb down off the stool and grab the bottom spoke, lift up and press down, which ever was necessary to keep the boat going on course. I brought this big ship down Boston Harbor to the army base, rang the bells for reverse and forward and secured alongside the pier. Of course, all the time the captain was standing right over my shoulder. That was a big thing for me and so I grew up with the attitude I didn't have to do anything to become a captain on the ocean. I always wanted to go to sea but because of the lack of guidance in those days, I didn't think I had to study and never realized the math that was needed. I should have studied but didn't so I never went to sea as a captain.

When we went to school in Salem, we came down on a police boat on Friday night so we had to drive to Atlantic Avenue in Boston. This particular Friday night the fireboat had replaced the police boat which had broken down. All of a sudden the fire alarm went off on the fireboat and we raced down the harbor. One of the lighthouses was burning - the Nubbles Island light (Narrows light and/or "Bugs Light" as we called it). It was a house and tower on stilts. They tried to get the dory off but in the excitement it was dropped too fast and one of the lines broke. The keeper got out on the end of the big pier and the fireboat dropped a boat over and took him off. The lighthouse keeper had been using a blowtorch to burn the paint off, which was common in those days. We watched them shooting water on the fire from the guns on the fireboat. They put the fire out but it was a total loss. Now all that remains is a steel beacon. So, instead of riding a fire engine, we rode the fireboat.

NARROWS (BUG) LIGHT
JUNE 7th 1929

On June 7, 1929, the Narrows (Bug) Light burned accidentally. I was on the fire boat coming home from school when the alarm came in and we raced down the harbor to watch them shooting water on the flames. The light was a total loss.

Dad would have a garden every summer on the island. During the winter months the waves from storms would splash over the seawall and fill the center part of the island. The center part of the island was very hollow and as the waves would fill in the center, the ground would bubble up. Air and oxygen would come up and it was almost like cultivating the garden. There was a French sailing vessel, the *Magnifique,* that ran aground in the 1700's. She was a pirate raider and had a lot of treasure. I don't know what ever happened to the treasure but there was always talk that the crew buried the money on the island.

Every spring, my Dad would dig up a coin and the oldest coin we have is dated 1600. So the treasure had to be buried there somewhere. No one knows where. There's a story that goes with it. The assistant keeper came to relieve Dad for a vacation and asked about the hole that had been dug in the garden. Dad showed two coins. Dad said jokingly, "That's where the treasure is buried". When Dad got back from vacation the hole was bigger and the assistant keeper retired a few months later. You can take it from there. I often wonder where my buried treasure is. As a lad, I put a note and some pretty stones from the beach into a tobacco can which I buried on the hill next to "Lovers Rock". I must go back some day and search.

This is a photograph of 8 coins that were dug out of our garden behind the house on the island. Some date back to the 1600's.

The range lights and kerosene house were connected by a trestle.

Chapter Seven

Time and trickery, the skunk and the biscuits, trained clams,When your boat is shipshape and turkeys and pheasants.

Above Left: The Army mules on the island in a corral. **Above Right** That's me on "Molly". All I had for a saddle was a burlap bag. When I went up the hill to the guns the motion of the mule caused the burlap bag to slip and I slid over the backside of the mule down to the ground. **Below:** My dog "Betsy" watching for the mail boat.

Chapter Seven:

On the island we also had army mules and we had a chicken wire fence around the garden to keep the chickens out. I had an eight day alarm clock that I had played with for years trying to make it run. One morning the mule got in the garden. Dad grabbed the alarm clock out of my play box in the back hall entrance and went out on the catwalk. He threw the clock and hit the mule right on the rump. A few days later, someone mentioned that my clock was still out in the garden and I should go out and get it. When I picked it up it was running. It ran for years after that. I also had a round clock - a horizontal clock - which looked like one dish on top of another but instead of the hand going around, the disk at the top part of the clock went around (like a music box). A school friend was visiting one time and we had just gone to bed when we heard my Dad hollering at us to get up. We could hear the stove covers being moved to light the morning fire. It was dark out as it was winter and I said to myself "I just went to bed, didn't I?" Charlie, my friend, was out in the hall trying to read this clock by the lamp light. Dad come up to the head of the stairs and tells us with a laugh that its only 10:30 p.m. - go back to bed! Just one of Dad's jokes.

Charlie was over another weekend and it was after supper and the stories started. On the middle of the dining room table was a goldfish bowl which had two goldfish in it. We had a bulldog and Dad said, "Charles, the other day a funny thing happened. Betsy (the bulldog) got in a living room chair and then up on the table (which was never allowed) and looked down inside the goldfish bowl. Being curious, I waited to watch what she was trying to do. Do you know what she did? Betsy put her paw down in the water, and scooped the fish out onto the table. Before I could get to the fish, Betsy gently picked it up again with her mouth and put it back in the bowl. What do you think of that?" Mom and I tried to keep straight faces. Sometime later, when I was back in school, Charlie's mother told me that Charlie had come home and told her this wild story about Betsy and the goldfish bowl. I assured her it was just one of Dad's tales.

Other stories dad would tell around the supper table included one about when he first joined the lifesaving station down in Cahoon's Hollow in Wellfleet (remember the bull?). Dad came home and told Mom that each man had to take his turn cooking and he said "I have to learn to cook." Mom said he didn't even know how to boil water. Mom made him some menus and he would go into town once a week and get a list of the dinners when it was his turn to cook. He began to enjoy cooking and the other guys didn't want to cook so he said "If you guys walk my beat on the beach, I'll cook." They were more than willing. In those days skunks were very valuable for their fur. In between dinners, Dad would see a skunk, trap it, skin it and dry the fur then sell it for fur coats. He had some pelts hanging behind the boathouse and one day he went out to the trash. Right by the corner of the building was a skunk. He rushed back into the station for his shotgun, shot the skunk twice but it kept running. Then when he went around the next corner he found two of the guys had wired together a skunk skin my dad had killed earlier, put a string on it and were running it around the corners of the building. They always played tricks on each other.

The captain of the station was always the first one down in the morning. He had to pass through the dining room to get to the washroom. Dad had just made a batch of biscuits and every time he made biscuits, the guys would snitch them on their way to the washroom. He would always be short by breakfast. One morning he took some biscuits, sliced them, slipped in some laundry soap and then marked them. All of a sudden, who comes down first? The captain. He grabs the top biscuit. Not a sound came from the washroom. Dad was sure he would get fired. Another seaman came along and took one - yet not a peep. One after the other. "Whats going on here?" thinks Dad. He removed the remaining biscuits with the soap and put some good ones on top again. At breakfast, no one ate any biscuits nor said anything. Finally, Dad assured them that there was no soap in the remaining biscuits. I guess they got the message because the biscuits didn't last long.

My uncle (Llewellyn Rogers) was a devil too, as far as characters go. Uncle Lew was keeper of Graves Light, which is on a granite rock outside of Boston and where there is no beach. He used to come to our light which is probably four or five miles from his light to dig clams. One summer day he had a bucket of clams sitting at the base of the tower. People came from Boston and wanted to visit the tower and he says "sure, come aboard." "Where did you get the clams?" somebody asked. He said, "There's a little story about those clams. I went over to a neighboring island a few years ago and I dug a bucket full of them. Once or twice a day I would bring a handful of

56

corn meal and dust it into the bucket and whistle. After a while, those clams would come right up to the top of the water to get the cornmeal. I had a bright idea - I dumped them over the side of the rocks here and every time I need a bucket of clams I take some cornmeal and I throw it on top of the water. Then I whistle and out comes the clams. I would then dip down and get a bucket full." People would want him to show them but he "didn't want to deplete his supply of clams." That's the story Uncle Lew would tell about the clams he raised among the rocks.

Lighthouse families seemed to be a close knit group. Uncle Lew wanted to be stationed on the south shore where the rest of his family were. He applied and fought for an appointment on Minots Light off Cohasset. The shore house was in Cohasset. He got the job in the spring. He rode out many nor'east storms that first winter. When spring came he made a plea with Captain Eaton (Second District Superintendent of Lighthouses) to please get his old station (Graves Light) back. He told us that the dishes were stored in holding racks like aboard a ship. When a winter wave hit the tower, the dishes would go "clink, clink". He went back to Graves Light.

Every once in a while, Dad made a point to come down to the dory when we were using it and make a personal inspection. In the dory we had to have an extra oar, extra plug (wooden for the drain hole), and anchor and enough line. Back in those days we did not have to have flotation devices (lifejackets). Today I feel lost in a boat without one.

On the island we didn't have any livestock. My folks raised turkeys called "bourbon reds" as well as chickens. They bought them through the poultry section of the Sears, Roebuck catalog. They were small turkeys and when they grew up some would get out over the fence. A turkey is well known for hiding. We had tall beach grass. One spring, the lady turkey who had escaped the turkey yard, would come out and eat her supper and go back to a nest in the deep grass. You would lose sight of her in no time flat. One time I went up in the tower and watched from the outside catwalk to see exactly where she went. She went in the tall beach grass, made a tunnel and weaved in and out for about ten feet. In there was her nest. At least we knew where the nest was and when the little ones came out we could capture them. They would have died otherwise if they got wet.

One of Dad's friends in Winthrop (Red Pierce) called him one morning and said, "Charles, I am sending you a pheasant for the island. When the mailboat came there was a box with holes and a "pheasant" in it. We went into the woodshed to let the "pheasant" out and to feed and water it. When we opened the box, what hopped out? - a bantam hen. I guess Dad's friend thought it was a pheasant. Once the bantam became broody so Dad put three turkey eggs in her nest. They hatched. Remember a bantam hen is larger than a duck but smaller than a hen. When the baby turkeys were a couple of weeks old, they were as large as the bantam. This caused a riot. When it was time for the hens to go to roost, the bantam would call them up to her roost. She would get one under her left wing and then coax the next one to get under her right wing. Now, there was one left over. She would call him to get under one or the other wings and when he did, mother hen would be pushed off the roost on to the floor of the hen house. This meant she would have to start all over again. Finally, she would give up and go to sleep. This bantam hen was getting old and Dad said, "we had better eat her before she gets tough." Dad tried to catch her but she was fast and Dad tripped and fell. He was so mad he got the twelve gauge shotgun and shot her. She was so small that all there was left was some feathers.

Speaking of those turkeys, when Dad took sick and Mom and I were running the Light Station, one day Mom said, "Son, you and I have got to kill a turkey." Out into the pen we went with me carrying a hatchet. Mom said she would hold the turkey. After a chase and a little wrestling, we caught the turkey we wanted. Mom had killed chickens in her day but not a big twenty pound turkey. With her arms wrapped around the turkey, we headed for the wood chopping block. When we got there, Mom said, "Pull her neck out onto the block and when she stops moving swing the ax and get out of the way." Well that turkey didn't want to die. I stretched the neck, swung the ax and three times the turkey pulled her head back (couldn't really blame her, could you?). Finally, I hit my target, jumped out of the way and Mom tossed the turkey to one side. Stepping back, she fell square on her backside. Just then, the turkey began to flap towards her before she could get up. I began to laugh. Mom yelled, "Get that darn thing away from me." But, I couldn't stop laughing. She never forgave me and often referred to "the time 'son' laughed at me while I was attacked by a turkey".

****

Chapter Eight

Captured, A trip to Provincetown on the steamer, The Banana Boat, Fishing boat tie up, the disappearing guns, the two targets-shirts etc., and friends picnicking on the island.

The United Fruit ship *San Blas.* This was the source of our free bananas now and then. Dad knew the Captain well. *Photo courtesy of the Steamship Historical Society collection at the University of Baltimore Library.*

Chapter Eight:

During the rum-running days, in the spring of 1933, a fishing boat, the *Annie C* from Provincetown was accused of picking up liquor while fishing off Cape Cod. The Coast Guard towed her from Provincetown to Boston where it got a little rough off Boston Light. One of the seamen got a line turned around his leg so they chopped her loose. It was getting late at night so they didn't bother to pick her up and she grounded on the back side of our island out towards Brewster Island. It was quite rocky and she punched a hole in her side when she laid over. The next morning when Dad went to the towers he saw her. The Coast Guard came down and boarded her. Soon after they left, I got into my row boat and rowed out. Everything of value had been stripped from her but one thing they missed was the compass which was jammed into the scuppers. I took it home and still have it.

I have told about blowing a police whistle and saluting boats that ran back and forth from Provincetown, New York and Savannah. The old *Dorothy Bradford* ran between Provincetown and Boston. One day we set out to visit Grandmother Jennings in Provincetown. We rode over to Quarantine Island, got on the Quarantine boat and went up to Boston in time to catch the "Dorothy Bradford" for Provincetown. On the way over, Dad met an old friend. Many years later, looking back I realized that this friend was Joseph C. Lincoln. I had been on boats my entire life - but the old *Dorothy Bradford* coming around Race Point rolled, and I mean rolled. I was getting kind of squeamish - I didn't like the way I felt. I told my Dad I was getting sick. He went to the stationary store on the boat and he bought a pad of lined paper. He told me to put one of the sheets down inside my shirt over my chest with the lines toward me. Don't ask me why but I didn't get seasick. In fact I felt better.

The United Fruit boat, the *San Blas,* came into Boston Harbor from time to time and my Dad knew Captain Kemp who wrote many sea stories. Every time the banana boat would come in to Boston, instead of going around to the big channel which we called the President Rhoades Channel, it would come in through the narrows. Dad would see it coming off Boston Light (we were right in the middle of all of the channels that came into Boston (see map). It was a pastime to take out the spyglass and identify the boats. No two ships were alike and you could identify them by silhouette. So when a banana boat came in we recognized it as the *San Blas* especially when a United Fruit boat came through the narrows. We knew that Captain Kemp would be aboard because he would come through the narrows just to give Dad bananas and say "Hi". We would get the dory, roll it down the beach and row out to meet him.

The banana boat would come in close between Lovell's Island and Quarantine (Gallops) Island. She would be flying a yellow flag (for the doctor on Quarantine Island to board and check the sick list). We couldn't go alongside until the yellow flag was taken down. She used to drift slowly. Slowly wasn't slow for one of those big boats as they had to keep moving in order to steer. Dad would estimate the time it would take to have the Quarantine doctor inspect her (because she had come from a foreign country), then approach on the starboard (right) side where there was a big door a few feet above the water line. The crew would open the door and hang a big stalk of bananas by a rope from a short beam waiting the OK to lower them to us. As soon as the yellow flag went down, Captain Kemp would give a couple of toots on the whistle and we would row close enough so they could lower the bananas into our dory as the two of us rowed like mad alongside this big ship. Dad and I always rowed together. Captain Kemp would come on the bridge and give a yell, "Hi Captain". Mom baked, fried and made bread for weeks from that huge stalk of bananas. A little comment on rowing: The dory you remember, was eighteen feet long and we used seven foot oars. I started rowing as soon as I could lift the two oars clear of the water (six or seven years old). Dad sat aft, I sat forward. This meant he set the stroke and I had to follow or our oars would tangle.

Fishing boats used to come from off shore. Dad was well known in the area (being from Provincetown) and well liked by all of the fishermen, many of whom he had fished with as a lad. They were not supposed to tie up at a government pier but they would tie up on Thursday nights, to wait for the market on Friday and be among the first boats in and get the best price for their catch. Sometimes they would be two or three deep and Dad would go down and yell, "Hey boys, you know you aren't supposed to tie up here - this is a government dock." "Hi Charles" they would say, "would you like a piece of swordfish? or maybe halibut?" There was a lot of bribery in those days, also, so they'd give a big hunk of swordfish and we'd have swordfish steak and the fishermen would be gone before daylight the next morning. One time, three of the fishing boats came out of Boston on their way to the fishing grounds and tied up at the pier for the night because of fog. The three boats had a party and they were feeling no pain.

When we went down early the next morning (they had overslept and had not left) they were all sprawled out on the boat sound asleep. On the deck were some full wine bottles. Three of us kids who were probably about fifteen years old at the time decided to take the ladder that was on the wharf, lower it down quietly, get the bottles of wine and run back up on the pier. Two of us tended the ladder and one went down. We got three bottles of wine which we would bring home to our Dads. We hid the bottles at the end of the pier and waited a little while. We came back down on the pier as though we had just gotten there and found that they had awakened. They were arguing about who had stolen their wine. They finally cast off to go fishing. My Dad was angry and said "those guys were drunk and would just as soon as knifed you as look at you." He warned us not to do such a thing again.

On the island there were four "batteries" which were cement casements covered with earth to hide the guns. These were World War I vintage guns. Two of the casements were disappearing guns. These guns as you can see by the picture, recoiled. They went up in the air, fired, and the firing kicked them back down. As soon as they came down, the breach was opened and another shell was put in along with a big bag of firing powder. A new cap put on the door, the door slammed and up it went in the air again. The gun sighter would look over the top of the casement with a periscope, sight the gun and set the range. The gun captain would pull the cord and the gun would go up in the air and come back down again just as quickly as it went up. During those times, we were warned not to go near the guns.

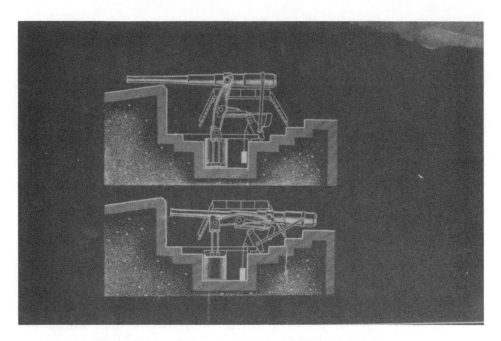

Above: A diagram showing the guns. The top illustration depicts the gun in the firing position. On the bottom, in the lower position. Hence, the term disappearing guns. **Below:** At Fort Pickens in the Gulf Shores Park, I am standing next to the big wheel that turned the gun around so us kids could ride. These guns were identical to the ones on Lovell's Island.

A close up view of the machinery on one of the guns at the Gulf Shores National Park in Pensacola, Florida.

Kid fashion, we sneaked up the back through the woods and over the top of the hill to the back part of the guns where we could look down into the casement and watch the action through the grass and not be seen. There was quite a recoil behind all this and the wind would blow your hair and the bushes around you. We had three of these six-inch guns near our house. Everyone on the island was warned to open their windows so that the vibration and concussion would not break the windows. There was a skeleton key in the back hall door keyhole and when the guns fired the key would jump out of the keyhole. That kept me out of my mother's hair for quite a while when I was a young kid.

The army (coast artillery) used to fire their anti-aircraft guns at a target towed by an airplane. At the end of the day, they would give empty shells away but I was never able to get one because "I was a kid". When the L-boat came into shallow water to pick up the target after they dropped it near the beach from the tow plane, sometimes they could not reach it. The L-boat would draw too much water so they would tow me around and I would put a hook into the target and then they would pull it up and drag it aboard the L-boat. One day I was mad because I couldn't get an empty bullet shell. At the end of the day, they towed me out but I told them I couldn't see that target, even though I really knew where it was. After they gave up and went home, I rowed out and hooked on to the target and towed it to the beach. It was silk, heavy and wet. I dragged it up and took it home. We had silk thereafter for many things. I don't know what my mother didn't use it for. So I got a target instead of a bullet out of that situation.

Everyone wondered when the plane flew over what tripped the tow target. You could see a ring going down the cable and pretty soon the target would get loose and away it would drift and come down on the island (or in the water). One day I was walking on the beach and I found a piece of rope with a ring sticking up out of the sand. I pulled it up and on the other end of it was a weight three-inches in diameter and weighing about three pounds. I took it up to the gun placement crew and showed it to them. After that no one stood out to watch the airplane come over and drop the target because that thing would have killed you if it hit you.

Once in a while they would let us up in the observation tower where they got their sightings and triangles. During this practice period (usually a week) a target was towed. Offshore, they towed a flat, wooden scow called a "sled", on top of which what looked like a big sailboat with red sails. They towed them way off shore (near Graves Light) and when the shipping got by they would shoot at these targets. They weren't supposed to score a direct hit (about 500-feet behind the target), but when the fellows wanted some time off they would hit the target and then it would have to come back and be rebuilt.

On the island after World War I, they cut down on the complements and there were only caretakers. There were three other families on the island besides us but they were up on the other end of the island. Their job was to keep the gun placements clean and be sure nobody broke into them. Keep the different generators running on the island in case the guns had to be used; and general maintenance. Once in a while, the families would have children stay on the island with them and I would have someone to play with. The disappearing gun placements had an archway to them which was as wide as a house. In the summer, it was cool there and my Mother would pack a lunch and we would have a picnic. We would make echoes and climb the steel ladder. We would imagine that we were part of the gun crew. Our favorite sandwich was peanut butter and jelly with home made root beer.

A crew working for the Army unloading six inch shells at the Army dock.

Looking at the breech of a six inch gun at the Gulf Shores National Park in Pensacola, Florida.

Chapter Nine

A radio in our lives with no electricity. A new washing machine for MomThe rum runners, salvaging storm tossed boats, guns in my life and the sights were off.

CONFIRMATION OF RECEPTION
OF

INTERNATIONAL TEST PROGRAM

Your reception of a program from

Station   2 LO

Located at   LONDON   ENGLAND

On Sunday, January 24, 1926

has been officially checked and attested to.

MUNSON T. ADAMS, Radio Editor

The Boston Herald—The Boston Traveler—The Sunday Herald

Official Publications for International Test Week

This is a copy of the document presented to my Dad by the Boston Herald and Boston Traveler.

Chapter Nine:

In the evenings, we sat around the radio and listened to "The Shadow", "Mandrake the Magician", "The Green Hornet" and "Little Orphan Annie". We listened to the speaker on top of the radio or used earphones so as not to annoy our parents. The radio was run by storage batteries like the car batteries of today. Dad made me a crystal radio set. It was made out of a round Quaker Oats box with wire wrapped around it and shellacked. On the top was a little rod that went back and forth. At one end where two wires went on, there was a little thing called a crystal. It had a little wire on the end of the rod and you rubbed it around on this crystal. I do not know how the devil it worked but believe it or not, with earphones you could get radio stations. This was called a "crystal set". Incidentally, my father received a certificate for catching an International System Radio broadcast on January 24, 1926. This program was put on by the Boston Herald and Boston Traveler. Everybody listened to the radio and the question was, "How far could a radio go?" The station that was received by my father was 2LO - London England.

We had no electricity but later on I will tell you about the power plant we had. How did we see? We used kerosene table lamps. Some with fancy shades for the living room and dining room and plain ones in the kitchen with glass globes on them with shades. We had small hand lamps to take upstairs with us when we went to bed. Dad answered an ad in Popular Mechanics and we got a wind generator. We picked a spot near the house on the northwest side and a twenty-foot "4 X 4" was used for the pole. (I say "we" because a lighthouse family did things together.) This generator had a two bladed propeller and purred like an airplane. It would charge storage batteries down in the basement on windy days. We would get six volts like today's car batteries, five or six in a row. The pole had a steel loop attached to it with a rope that you could pull down and keep the wind generator from going by putting the blade in a horizontal position called "tripping the generator". This was so if the wind got too strong and the batteries got up too much charge you could shut it off. Dad bolted the generator to the twenty-foot pole and with a little help from Mom and me the pole was up with the generator on top. The necessary wires hung from the generator to the batteries in the cellar. My Dad had three six-volt bulbs. One in the living room, one at the head of the stairs and one in the kitchen. We had electric light now! Wow! We all knew at this time how Thomas Edison felt when he lit his first light bulb.

71

One night after we had our lights, the three families from the other end of the island came to admire our new lights. As I mentioned, the rope was used to trip the generator in high winds so it wouldn't break the propeller and cause the whole thing to fly apart. One Friday, we all went to Boston on the mailboat to do some shopping. While we were gone, the west winds came up and they were real strong. The generator should not have been kept running as the winds were too strong and when we got home the old generator was reving up and shaking the pole like mad. Dad said, "All three of us are going to have to try to pull the generator through the wind and put it in neutral." We pulled and tugged but it kept vibrating worse and worse. "Lets get out of here, if that prop comes off who knows where it will go". That evening we were not allowed to go into the living room as the pole was about eye level with the windows. The next morning, all was well except the prop had only one blade. (The blade must have ended up in Boston harbor.) After the batteries ran down, we were back to the good old table lamps.

The next big event was when Dad surprised Mom with a gasoline driven washing machine (from Sears Roebuck) with a motor just like a modern day lawn mower. All of a sudden I became interested in washing clothes. Why? Wouldn't you if all you had to do was jump on the thing like a motorcycle and away it would start. It was a lot of fun for a kid to get that washing machine whizzing around. Before this "modern machine" the laundry was done in the cellar in a two compartment soap stone set tub. The laundry was carried up a flight of seven stairs and then down the same number of steps to the ground to be hung out. As I have mentioned, the house was on a seven-foot foundation. During the time of the six-volt system and the washing machine, I was about ten or twelve years old. Before the new washing machine with the gasoline engine, we would wring the clothes with a crank which was along side the set tub. The tighter the clamp, the drier the clothes got. That was my job if I happened to be around when Mother was doing the laundry. When I look back, it seemed Mom managed to make sure that I was around on Monday "washday" (except when I was away at school).

You have all heard of prohibition and the rum-running days. During this time the big boats came into the harbor from international waters, got custom seals and would go back out. This was okay as long as they didn't leave any rum. One night we heard a speedboat go around the island and all of a sudden it stopped outside the breakwater and then took off. The next morning there was this funny looking buoy out there which wasn't common to the area. My father said, "Come on Son, lets go get the dory and pull

This is a typical rum runner during the days of prohibition. The NOLA was equipped with fast engines and protected by steel plates. *Photo courtesy of the National Archives, Washington, D.C.*

that buoy." My mother said, "You keep away from there - you know what it is and if they catch you they'll run you down for stealing their booze." My father said "We'll be careful." So we launched the dory and we both rowed out. As we were coming around the point of the island, we saw a speedboat coming out of Boston. We stopped rowing and the speedboat sped around near the breakwater, pulled up the buoy and zipped back to Boston with it.

Dad sure was disappointed. He wasn't a heavy drinker but liked to have it on hand for guests. One night we heard another speedboat racing around the island. It would stop, then it would race around the island again and stop. Then come back around the island and stop. All of a sudden, a seaplane came out of Boston and tried to find the boat with the plane's headlight. The boat turned out its lights and they never did find them. One of the rum-runners had a trained seal on deck and it was said they dropped the rum over the side of the boat with a short buoy on it. The seal would later dive down and snatch the buoy and bring up the bag of booze which was attached to it.

The land areas surrounding Lovell's island are Hull, Quincy, South Boston, East Boston, Boston, Lynn and Salem. Boats would break away from moorings during storms and I would see them out in the water partially sunk or drifting. I used to row out and drag them on the beach. The police boat would come down and check their reports on missing boats, some of which we had found. I was given a reward once for an old fashion duck boat used for hunting. The owner must have thought the world of it and I got a five dollar bill which was big money in those days.

Once, I found a fourteen foot sailboat with a wooden mast but no sail. We ran an ad in the paper and told the harbor police about it but no one claimed it. I finally got by Mother to sew a sail for it and I sailed it during the summer of '38. One day in August, my Dad made his usual inspection of the boat and said, "Son, you've got to get rid of this boat - its not safe". So I put an ad in the Hull paper and got $20 for it. Dad couldn't believe anyone would pay $20 for that old boat. I actually bought my first boat with $110 I got when I worked for the lighthouse service for a month as a substitute for my Dad when he was sick. (The next month the hurricane of '38 wrecked the old boat I had sold.) I found an outboard speed boat and I fixed it all up - scraped and varnished it and had it for some time hoping I could get a motor for it, which I never did. I finally sold it.

When my friends came to the island a big event was to fire the shotgun which my father pretended had a big kick. Of course, Dad had to fire the gun first. He would fire it up in the air and stagger back as though he was going to fall. "What a kick!!" he would say, and then would hand the gun to my visiting friend. "Brace yourself - hold the gun tight to your shoulder, aim and squeeze the trigger slowly," he would say. I always felt sorry for my visiting friend but I would say nothing. He would do what he was told and off goes the gun - he would look at me and say, "that wasn't bad". Dad would laugh, "just trying to scare you" he would say. Dad always had a shotgun and a rifle in the house. There were guns in the closet and shells in the bureau drawer in the hall, all of which had a "don't touch" warning (which he meant).

I finally received my first gun - a B-B gun. I think I grew up a couple of years at the moment it was handed to me. Dad would say, "This gun is to be handled as if it were a high-powered shotgun or rifle and remember this and every gun is 'always loaded' even if there is not a single B-B or shell in it. If you misuse this or any other gun you may own I will personally wrap the gun around a tree." He was a man of his word, and I knew it. I had to clean it after every use and care for it just like it was any other caliber rifle.

Later in my life I received a 22 caliber rifle (single shot) after I had proved myself with the B-B gun. With a six foot fence in the back of the house, it was great to line up tin cans as targets. One time, during the winter months, my Dad finally allowed me to use his 12 gauge shotgun and I decided to go on a goose hunt. There were geese out back on the bar so I climbed over the rocks crawling on my belly. It was cold. I crept cautiously so as not to scare them. I was just about ready to set the shotgun up to by shoulder and shoot one of the geese sitting close by when a gull saw me and started squawking. All of the geese left. I fired but didn't get a darn thing.

Many of my father's hunting stories (always told when the guns came out) had to be taken with a grain of salt - like this one: "I bought a used shotgun from a fellow who said it was a little off on the sights. I went down to the shore on the back side on the island where all of the ducks come in to rest and figured I would get me a couple for tomorrow's dinner. There in front of me as I climbed over the seawall was the biggest flock of ducks I had ever seen. Being a good sportsman, I always believed in shooting my ducks in flight. So I readied the new shotgun. I yelled and every duck took off and circled to the south and turned right back towards me so I could get the best shot a hunter could ask for. I aimed, fired, and then tried to remember which way the sights were off. I found out in a few minutes because all of a sudden I had no ducks but I had a barrel of legs. Sights must have been too low".

The Boston Lightship on station twelve miles east of Boston. The ship was replaced by a large buoy in May of 1975. After 79 years, the Boston Lightship was retired.

Chapter Ten

Mine practice and fishing, lobstering, and a thrilling moment. A tug of war, inspection time, the wrong paint and fire around the big tower.

Above Left: Dad cleaning one of the glass windows on the light. **Above Right** This is a snapshot of me when I was eight years old. **Below:** Thats me rowing in my dory.

Chapter Ten:

Earlier, I wrote about the "L" boats. They were used as mine layers and the Army would practice in July. They ran big electrical cables about an inch in diameter. The cables would be towed from the beach on Georges Island (Fort Warren) and taken out towards Boston Light in between the channels and mines would be fastened to these cables. (This went on between World Wars I and II.) They would put the mines out, tow a target over the top and blow up the target from the control tower on Fort Warren. When the mines blew up, it would stun the fish. They would come to the surface and float for a while until they got the air out of their gills. Then they would sink down again. About 4:00 p.m., when we knew they were going to fire the last time, we would row along the east edge of our island over towards "Bugs Light" and lay up alongside the sandbar. When the red flag came down over Fort Warren we knew that mine practice was over so we rowed across the channel to the area where the last mine had gone off and picked up cod and flounder for supper.

It was an easy way to fish. In late summer and early fall we would fish the holes that the mines had made as the fish went down in there to hide from the currents and feed. It was nice fishing. Dad would tie the anchor in a special way - tying a line around the fluke - the front end of the anchor from the ring - run it over the top of the ring (not through it) and take a piece of cord line and tie it down to the ring because once in a while you would hook on to one of these cables and you couldn't get the anchor loose. So as not to lose an anchor, you would have to get the cable up as high as you could and my father would cut the cord line with his knife and the anchor would trip and drop the cable. Dad lost a couple of anchors by saying, "I won't get hung up this time".

We were allowed five lobster traps and when I got older - probably about fourteen or fifteen - Dad allowed me to have my five lobster traps and we would get crabs and lobsters all summer. In those days we took this for granted - lobster every day if we were lucky. The first time I saw a spider crab (resembles a big spider) in my lobster trap, it was the ugliest thing I had ever seen and so I whistled for Dad with my police whistle. He came down, reached in the trap, assured me it wasn't as dangerous as it looked and threw it away because they weren't good to eat.

One time when our piano needed tuning, my Dad contacted someone in Boston and the gentleman who came was blind. This was in July when the mackerel were running good. The blind man tuned the piano for us and while we were waiting on the pier for the boat to come to take him back to Boston, we decided to try to catch some mackerel. We used bamboo poles about fifteen feet long with a mackerel jig attached to the end of a line which stretched from the top of the pole to about where your hand held the pole. You would swing it over your head, slowly pick the end of the pole up and jiggle the mackerel jig across the water and the mackerel would bite it. We would pull the pole up on the pier with an over the shoulder swing and the mackerel would fall off the hook onto the pier. I can remember watching this blind man when the pole was put in his hands. After Dad taught him the motions, he caught a mackerel. You should have seen this man as he felt the fish. He was so pleased with what he had caught - a moment I never forgot. We wrapped the fish in newspaper so he could take it home with him.

Dad used to split mackerel and salt them down. By the next spring, the salt had all gone to the bottom of the barrel and most of the mackerel were "rusted" and no good. As kids, we would take two mackerel and tie a five or six foot string around each tail, throw them down on the beach and watch the sea gulls. One gull would get ahold of one mackerel and another would grab the other mackerel. The gulls would go their separate ways. There would be a catastrophe as the gulls could only fly a short way because the mackerel were attached to each other. Didn't hurt the gulls, just aggravated them.

Captain Eaton was superintendent of the second district and the inspector of lighthouses for the district which encompassed Boston and surrounding lighthouses. He and Dad knew each other very well and were old buddies but they had a running feud trying to "get something" on each other. From our house, we could see all of the boats coming out of Boston Harbor. It was a morning routine to take out the spyglass, go out on the porch and scan the harbor for anything that could be seen. About 8:00 or 9:00 a.m. you would see business boats, towboats and lighthouse tenders working on the buoys and delivering supplies to lighthouses, etc. Dad would look through his spyglass at the tenders as they came down from Chelsea and say: "No inspection today - all of the buoys are on deck and the workboat is hung out and ready to go to work." He could identify a lighthouse tender by its name which was usually a plant or flower such as *Locust, Shrub, Mayflower* and the *Azelea.*

The Lighthouse steamer *Shrub*.

On this particular day, the *Shrub* was coming down out of Boston. There were no buoys on deck. All boats and gear were secured but there was no inspector's flag flying. Dad said, "Hmmm - here comes that Eaton - he's going to pull a trick inspection. Well, he's not going to get me - I'll fix him." When he told me to go out and play somewhere I knew Dad was up to some of his deviltry. Dad put his overalls on, went out in the shed, mixed some paint and started painting along the trestle with his back to the pier (which was midway on the island). As the lighthouse tender quietly moved into the pier, up went the inspector's flag and Captain Eaton came off the boat with his first mate. They came down the road towards the tower. As they came up the catwalk (trestle), Dad's back was to them and he was painting on the trestle like mad. Captain Eaton came up behind Dad and said: "Captain Jennings?" Dad turned around looking surprised and said, "Oh, Captain Eaton, how are you?" Captain Eaton responded, "How come you aren't in uniform?" and Dad answered, "How come you didn't fly a flag?" Here they go again. The Captain said, "Look, I have a flag up," and Dad said, "Yeah, you flew it the minute you came into the pier. I'm not going to get dressed for you if you're not going to fly a flag while you're underway." Then Dad would write in the log that the tender came down without an inspector's flag flying.

Once, when Captain Eaton came down for inspection, everything was official - the flag was flying and Dad had his uniform on. This time the inspection started in the house. Dad came out of the house with me trotting behind him. The first mate was up inside of the tower. Dad stomped down from the house and hollered up the tower, "Get your fanny down from that tower." Captain Eaton said, "But he's my first mate." "I don't care who he is - he didn't have permission from me to go into that tower. I'm the keeper here." That was the way they went back and forth at each other but they were always buddies at the end, passing cigars out to each other, pats on the back, "Charles" this, and "Eaton" that.

Another time, Dad had just painted the inside of the house when Captain Eaton inspected it. Dad didn't want to put up wallpaper so he stippled the walls with a sponge and and old fashion paint printer (to make fake knots, etc.). Government rules said you could only use certain approved combinations of colors. The sponge looking effect going up the hallway made a pretty wall but Captain Eaton was up and down that wall trying to find a color that wasn't legal. Dad said: "You can search from here to high water but you won't find a color that isn't legal", and Captain Eaton never was able to find an illegal color.

As I have mentioned before, the army was on the island. The army had a rifle range there and during the summer, groups like the National Guard would come down and fire on this range. The National Guard of Boston decided to fly down and have some machine gun practice from a plane. Back in those days, gunners shot out of the rear cockpit and they were just studying how to shoot through the propeller. This particular day every tenth bullet was a tracer bullet (so they could follow their aim from the front cockpit). One bullet accidentally set the grass on fire. The few people that were on the island fought the fire but it came close to the towers and singed some of the paint on the lower part of the shingles. Nothing bad, but it did mean a report had to be filed and Captain Eaton came to make the inspection and go over the fire rules.

This time, instead of docking the tender, Captain Eaton had his crew row him ashore in a deep keeled rowboat. Our beaches were sandy and shallow. Captain Eaton was standing up on the bow of the rowboat which was about five or six feet from the high-water mark and aground, hollering at the crew to "row, row, row!" I yelled, "Captain Eaton, why don't you get down in the back of the boat?" He responded with a "Humph" and climbed to the back of the boat. This was Dad's opportunity and he shouted, "By God, the kid knows more about boats than you do, Eaton." This was an example of the little digs at each other. Captain Eaton came ashore. Dad was in his uniform because, having seen the flag on the boat, he knew he was coming. They went up to the tower and discussed whether the fire extinguishers were full, and the whole inspection routine.

Captain Eaton smoked cigars. As he and Dad went around the lee of the tower to return to the tender, Captain Eaton lit his cigar and threw the match down. As they were walking down to the beach, Dad happened to look back to see that grass around the tower (not burned in the previous fire) was on fire. They ran back and Dad hollered to Captain Eaton, "Give me your jacket." Without thinking, Captain Eaton took off his uniform jacket and handed it to Dad who proceeded to beat the grass with it. Captain Eaton hollered, "That's my uniform." Dad said, "Well, you started the fire." After the fire was put out, Captain Eaton, with a buddy-buddy attitude, said "Now, Charles, we're going to forget this little episode, aren't we?" Dad said, "No we're not! - I'm going up to the house and put this report in the log." "You wouldn't do that, would you Charles?" This exchange went on as they climbed the ladder and went across the catwalk to the house with Captain Eaton right on Dad's tail. Dad was anxious to get to the log to write it all down, which he did. This was another "I got you" episode.

Dad relaxing after an inspection tour with Captain Eaton.

The Lovell's Island range lights in June, 1934.

Chapter Eleven

Lighthouse stills, a special Thanksgiving.
Celebrating the fourth ofJuly, the rifle range and
manning the targets.

An aerial photograph of Boston light station taken in February, 1989.

Chapter Eleven:

I'll tell you a little story about moonshining during the Prohibition years in the 1930's. Dad and Mom made malt beer. In the hallway which led from the kitchen to the front door there was a type of pantry that had drawers on the lower part, a space in the middle with draw curtains and above it, glass like a china closet. In this area, Dad had a five gallon crock in which he put his malt beer while it was brewing. All of a sudden, one day, Captain Eaton is coming down the harbor and the flag is flying. Dad grabbed the five gallon crock and with a cloth covering it, ran out the door, down the stairs and out into the woods where he set the crock down. Mom got the flit gun (a pump sprayer used to kill flies) out and sprayed the area to try to eliminate the smell of the malt. It was against the law to have home brew or alcohol on a station. I thought this was all great fun as I was sworn to absolute secrecy.

Over on the Deer Island Light, things didn't work out too good for two fellows who had a vat going when the inspector came. This lighthouse was like a big barrel out in the middle of the bay with a catwalk all the way around it. When the inspector came up the ladder from the rowboat, one of the keepers was on one side of the tower with his arms wrapped around a five gallon crock. When the inspector asked the keeper where the assistant keeper was, the keeper replied, "I took him ashore for a little while and have to go back to get him later this afternoon." As the keeper and the inspector circled the tower, the assistant keeper managed to keep out of sight by walking around just ahead of them. There was a lightning rod that came from the top of the tower, down the side of the tower, across the catwalk and down into the ground to the water. As the assistant keeper walked around the tower with the crock in his arms, he tripped over the lightning rod and the malt spilled all over as the crock crashed to the deck. The inspector ran around the tower and the assistant keeper was caught. He was fired. This homemade malt was not as strong as some of the stuff that was being smuggled back in those days - it was a mild drink - but it was still illegal, especially on government property.

87

We've talked about Christmas so now let's talk about other holidays. On Thanksgiving, I would be home from school. If Dad wasn't able to get a goose, we had a turkey - I think a couple of times we had ham. Dad would always try to get a wild goose - one year we even had wild duck. This particular Thanksgiving we had turkey. It was a windy Thanksgiving day - the wind was coming from the southwest at gale force. The next island to us was the quarantine island (Gallop's Island) which was where the crew from foreign ships came while their ship were being fumigated - especially if they came from certain parts of Africa. The crew stayed in barracks on the island while their ship was being fumigated.

This Thanksgiving, there was a British ship in quarantine and the crew was playing soccer. With the wind, the soccer ball went overboard and two of the crew started after the ball in a rowboat. Due to the wind and tide, they got involved and Dad noticed they were in distress. He went down to the beach and hollered to them to row over to our islands which was downwind from where they were. They rowed to our island and he took them up to the house as they were cold and wet. He called the quarantine station to tell them that it was too windy for the sailors to row back and said he would like to have them for dinner. So, the station said they would pick them up later. It was very interesting to me that these two young men didn't know what Thanksgiving was. These British sailors enjoyed our meal and it was educational for me as well as them as they talked to us about England and we told them about Thanksgiving.

On the fourth of July, I usually tried to get someone from the mainland that I had gone to school with to come over and some of my cousins might also come down. We would spend our time scrounging the beach and going out to the northwest corner of the seawall where we would pile up all kinds of boxes, barrels, driftwood and anything else we could find to make a pyramid of wood. On the evening of the fourth of July, we would set fire to this pyramid built at the end of the breakwater. We used to have some pretty good roaring fires. Dad would fire off the "2 inchers" as they were called and we kids were allowed to fire off the "Lady Fingers" and light the rockets. On Halloween, we would put a pumpkin out on the porch with a candle on it and sit around telling ghost stories while having the usual halloween candies and lemonade.

July fourth reminds me of the rum-running days again. Dick (George) Jennings, my cousin from Provincetown, came down to visit one fourth-of-July. The rum-runners were coming in and out hiding behind ships as they came into Boston. One night the *Dorothy Bradford* coming from Provincetown was late. It was about dusk and we went down to the breakwater at the end of the seawall to give them a three blast salute on my little police whistle. We didn't realize that a speedboat was traveling behind the *Bradford* close to her stern. The ship had responded with three blasts to my salute and all of a sudden this speedboat stopped and, in the reflection of the setting new moon across the water, was this boat with some crates on top just drifting and laying idle. Dick and I got scared and we ducked down behind the rocks and didn't dare move, imagining that they would shoot at us if we moved. Dad was calling to us but we didn't dare to answer. Finally, Dad came down on the breakwater yelling, "Where are you kids?" We told him what happened. In the meantime the speedboat started up and took off again. We probably scared them more than they scared us but we weren't going to take any chances.

There was a target range on the island, and in the summer months they used to shoot with 30-0-6 rifles and some machine guns. After they through firing for the day, we kids would pick up all the shells and clips from the machine guns to make belts out of them, wrapping them around us by the dozens until we looked like bandits with ammunition belts. We had a lot of fun with those machine gun belts. Also, while they trained for the week or two, we would go over to the mess hall next to the old engineer house and mooch dinners. It was a great treat to sit there with all the soldiers and share their prepackaged sandwiches, usually ham and cheese.

In the summer months, the island was also used as a picnic area. The Elks from Winthrop used to have their annual picnic on the island. I have a picture showing all the Elks present at one picnic. We used to get tips for showing them around the island. When the picnic was over, they didn't bother taking all the food back so we would try to bundle up all the remaining food we could carry home. We always ate pretty good after an Elks picnic.

Talking about target practice, further back I mentioned the tower catching on fire, which was caused by the flying National Guard. The flying guard had two wing planes (biplanes) and they would fire out of the cockpit at a long rectangular target on the ground which was about eight by twenty feet. My family would have to watch to make sure there were no boats on the back side of the shore, so we had a big cloth lying on the ground that had a white side and a red side. If we saw a boat coming within the range of the airplanes that were diving onto the island, we would turn the cloth red until the boat had gone past the back part of the island. When the plane was through firing, it would fly over the house, rock its wings and we would then go out with a paint can and color all the holes in the target - painting them so we could tell each of the plane's score.

Through our efforts, I used to get all of my ammunition for my 22 caliber rifle. When a plane was coming down, they would call and ask how my 22's were holding up and then drop a box of five hundred shells for me to use, so I never had to buy any ammunition. I have some aerial tubes that were dropped with long trailing flags on them that carried notes to my folks telling them what they were going to do and thanking them for the coffee when the crew had come down by boat to visit one time. I had the opportunity to go up in one of the planes and fly over Boston. As these were open cockpit planes, it was quite a thrill for me as a young lad as I wore a large leather helmet and goggles. Dad was asked if he wanted to go up in another plane and fly along with us. "No way," said Dad. "Only if I can keep one foot on the ground, will I go up."

The *SS City of Columbus* of the Savannah Line went ashore on Lovell's Island on March 10, 1921. Five tugs towed the ship off the beach. There was some bottom damage to the steamer. *Photo courtesy of Bob Beattie, Belfast, Maine.*

Chapter Twelve

Shipwrecks around Boston harbor, the race is on, an automobile. The attacking eagle and winter sports.

Above: The *City of Salisbury* on Graves ledge with a Coast Guard cutter anchored nearby. **Below:** The ship broke in half and the stern half remained on the rock for a long period of time before it sank. At the top of the photograph on the right is Graves Lighthouse.

The *City of Salisbury* with a salvage barge alongside. The ship had a cargo of exotic wild animals aboard. Monkeys, trumpet birds, pythons and several deadly cobras. Much of the animal cargo was saved but there was a large loss of her cargo of rubber and jute in the holds. The ship went aground in dense fog on April 22, 1938.

Chapter Twelve:

During my eighteen years on the island, there were a number of shipwrecks. Of two that are outstanding in my memory, one was the wreck of the *City of Salisbury*. She ran up on a pinnacle of rock and sank off Graves Light and debris started floating ashore. There were bales of rubber, bales of cotton, crates of tea and supposedly, Persian rugs which were never located. I found a little wicker basket and inside of it were waste scrap rags and in the middle of the rags were three little white tablets. I was always taught never to taste anything I found on the beach - just bring it home if there was any question. Come to find out, at the time of the sinking of the *City of Salisbury* (a British ship coming from India) when they were taking the crew off, one of the crew lost his basket overboard and was very much concerned about it. I didn't realize at the time but even back in those days they were looking for drugs. Dad was curious about the tablets so he called the harbor police and they stopped by. They found what they were looking for, relating the basket I found, to the basket that was lost by the crew member, they had the evidence they needed.

The steamer *Romance* was sunk in a collision with the *New York* in Boston harbor. *Photo by R. Loren Graham, courtesy of the Steamship Historical Society collection at the University of Baltimore Library.*

In those days, Indians loaded and unloaded the ships of British registry and they were very underpaid. We got $5.00 a bale for the rubber. We kids couldn't roll the rubber because the bales were so big - 150 pound bales. When we saw them on the beach, we would get help from Dad and the army people who would put ropes around the bales and get the old car to pull them up and thus get money for salvage. They didn't want the tea salvaged so when we found a 150 pound box of tea we would break it open and bring it to the boathouse. The ladies (including my mother) would put big sheets down on the floor of the boathouse and spread the tea out to dry. Then divide it up. It was good tea. Coconut came ashore in 150 pound boxes. I thought I would never want to see another shred of coconut in my life. We would have coconut in everything. I found one box - a crate. I waded out and dragged the crate out of the water and ran home for help. It turned out that in the crate were two five gallon cans of raw cashew nuts. Again, we had cashew nuts in everything we ate. So quite a bit resulted from the *City of Salisbury* wreck. She lay quite a while on this pinnacle of rock which they claimed was uncharted, yet the pilots knew it was there. But it was foggy and they hit this pinnacle. The vessel hung on there for a number of years. I remember going out there and just the stern was showing. The big waves would go inside and blow out the vent pipes. It made a big roar. Finally, she rolled over and disappeared from sight.

The Boston to New York steamer *New York* underway. *Photo by R. Loren Graham, courtesy of the Steamship Historical Society collection at the University of Baltimore Library.*

The other accident involved the Eastern Steamship Company's *New York* which ran between Boston and New York City and took the "Narrows" out by Boston Light and then come down through the Cape Cod Canal. The *SS Romance* ran from Provincetown to Boston. The *Romance* would leave in the morning and come back in the afternoon. The *New York* would come in in the morning and go out in the afternoon. The *Romance* was coming from Provincetown one late afternoon when it was foggy. She had two hundred passengers on board and the Captain decided that because the *New York* was due to come through the narrows, he would instead go out around Graves Light and come in through the main ships' channel, "the President Roads". In the meantime, the Captain of the *New York* decided rather than get tangled up with the *Romance* in the narrows, he would go out "the President Roads" channel.

The two boats collided off Graves Light. The *New York* hit the mid section of the *Romance*. The Captain of the *New York* was smart enough to keep pushing and then a single ladder was put over the bow and two-hundred passengers were brought safely over the bow and on to the deck of the *New York*. Then when the *New York* backed up, the *SS Romance* sank to the bottom. I have a soap dish from the *Romance.* As far as other shipwrecks, they were usually small boats - one boat got its stern cut by a fishing boat and everybody was saved but they had to drag the boat into our pier. It was a yacht. It sank and stayed there for quite a while until someone came and patched the stern and temporarily floated it away to Boston to be repaired.

The four stack destroyer *U.S.S. Paulding, CG17* returning to Boston after the collision with the submarine S-4 off Provincetown. I shot this picture with my 120 Box Brownie.

Looking back in history, the submarine *S-4* was sunk off Provincetown by the Coast Guard cutter *Spaulding*, number 17. I can remember hearing on the radio in the morning that the destroyer #17 was returning to Boston. I had a little box camera and went down to the south end of the island where I would be closest to her when she came in through by Bugs Light in the narrows. I sat on the shore until she arrived and got a picture of her. You could see the cut in her bow from the collision.

Another rescue involved a boat that was wrecked on Calf's Island off the outer Brewsters. The army boat, *General Anderson*, was going to try to rescue them but had no lifeboat to lower to go get them. They came over to get Dad and our dory. I remember going with him and we went out to Calf's Island and they towed the dory out. We carried the men from the island to the *General Anderson*. My Dad received a citation on this occasion also. My part in this rescue was to help Dad put the dory in through the rocks. He preferred me over any of the crew from the *Anderson* because the crew members were soldiers. Some who had never seen the ocean until they came to Boston. We rowed to the rocks where the small boat was stranded. Then Dad threw an anchor over the stern of our dory and had me hold a strain around the stern seat. When he wanted to move in toward the rocks, he would have me play out the line. All this time he was steadying the dory with the oars. As we neared the rocks, one at a time the three men jumped in. The Captain of the *Anderson* was a well qualified seaman but could not leave his ship to help. I was always proud and ready to go. At this time, I was only ten years old. An example of the deck crews ability was shown one day when the *L-48* went aground and the *L-52* went to take off the mail. Two soldiers got into the double ended life boat and sat back to back, arguing which end was the bow. Again, Dad and I came to the rescue.

96

Above The *SS Steel Pier,* excursion boat running from Boston to Provincetown. *Photo post card courtesy of Clive Driver, Provincetown, Mass.* Below: The *SS Dorchester* of the Savannah Lines leaving Boston. Another photo I made with my 120 Box Brownie.

There was a lot of controversy between the Provincetown excursion boats. The *Steel Pier* was running at the same time the *SS Romance* was running. The two boats were given permission to land in Provincetown and by some fluke, the pier was leased to both boats and it was a matter of who got there first as there was room for only one boat. I saw some hair- raising moments there in Boston Harbor when those two boats would leave in the morning and race for Provincetown. Its a wonder somebody didn't get hurt but they were only close calls. They couldn't do it today and get away with it.

The *Dorchester* of the Savannah Lines used to go by our house in the morning on the way up from the Carolinas. She was used as a troopship during World War II and was lost with so many on board when she was torpedoed. It was reported that the clergymen on board gave their own lifejackets away to the soldiers.

As I mentioned, my folks would take the old car and tow the bales of rubber up on the beach. This "old car" was a 1928 Hudson. Dad bought it over in Hull. On a calm day, the army L-boat went to the Hull pier and the Hudson was rolled on to the forward deck where it just about fit across the boat. When they got to our pier, they put the planks across and drove the car onto the pier. I was fourteen years old and Dad taught me to drive, with one warning. "Don't ever drive that car on to the pier!" Like all children, I forgot this warning one Friday when Dad had gone uptown shopping and I wanted to surprise him by having the car parked on the pier waiting for his return. I made it with no problems - none until Dad got off the boat and asked, "Who drove the car onto the pier?" Proudly, I said, "I did, Dad." Wow, I received one of Dad's few tongue lashings and was grounded as far as driving this car for a period of time.

When I was about three or four years of age, we kids used to play under the porch where it was always sandy and cool during the day. One day my Mother heard this awful squawking noise and when she went out by the porch to investigate, there was a great big eagle with his head down between the porch and a railing. The other wing caught under the other railing and it looked like he was trying to get down to where we were. My Mother ran down to the garden to get a pitchfork, ran back up the stairs, took the pitchfork and pinned the eagle to the deck. She killed the eagle and when they measured the wing spread it was seven feet. I don't know whether the eagle was after us or why he was in that position but he had gotten his wing caught inside the railing of the catwalk and Mom was scared for us.

In the winter, we used to come home on the weekends if the island wasn't iced in. There would be big snowdrifts off the hills. Another lad and I started a project. We took some barrel staves and some boards to make ourselves a double runner toboggan. We would struggle pulling it up the hill through deep snow until one day, on the way down, it fell apart. Our nailing and our principle of steering wasn't quite strong enough to stand the motion of going down hill. Back to the drawing board and we decided to make skis. The barrel staves weren't that slippery so it made for kind of rough skiing. The toboggan was our best vehicle - we had some good rides down that long hill of the gun emplacement right down into the swamp in the middle of the island. We would ice skate there also. I can remember a pair of four bladed skates I had. I got stuck out on the ice one time and started one of my screaming tantrums. Mom came to the scene and found out I was okay - just mad. Her response to my predicament was typical: "If you can't skate back, CRAWL!", which was what I finally had to do to get off the ice. Mom was a great teacher of self confidence.

Chapter Thirteen

Seven tons of coal, our fuel oil and the self planting gardens.Lobster bait, a Nor-easter, dredging the army dock, the seawall and the tunnel.

Frenchie, our cat on the front porch with the small light tower in the background.

Chapter Thirteen:

In the early fall, we would have a shipment of coal. We used seven tons of coal a year in our stove and furnace. The coal was brought from the tender on to a working rowboat, brought ashore and piled up on the beach. The tender's crew were dark-skinned, most were from the Cape Verde islands, they would chant and sing. I used to love to sit and watch them come up the beach. Each one would have a 50 to 60 pound bag on his shoulder. The bags were thrown up through a window to fill the coal bin. Remember, the house was seven feet above the ground. One day they were unloading and singing and chanting as usual. Remember the Persian angora cat, "Frenchie". The cat came out from the corner of the building and I don't know what they thought he was but the bags dropped like dominoes and they started running for the boat. We couldn't figure what was the matter with them. The first mate yelled at them and told them to get back to work as they were all trying to get into these two rowboats to go back to the mother ship. Finally, I picked the cat up not knowing the cat was the cause of the trouble and then the crew calmed down.

It took approximately five-hundred gallons of oil a year for the oil lamps at that time. There was a big 500-gallon oil tank outside the house on the beach above high water. My Dad would lug the oil from the tank in five gallon cans and put them in the woodshed. From them, he would fill a one gallon can to take up to the tower each night. We had a wood stove in the kitchen - we burned coal and wood. Wood was the primary heat source. We had a big two wheel army push cart that we used when we went along the beach to pick up our wood. Each person on the island did the same thing and when we walked the beach we each made little piles until the pickup day. They were sacredly kept - no one tried to steal. We stacked the wood in the wood shed to be used during the winter months (along with coal).

Garbage was thrown overboard from passing ships and in the spring up would come a tomato or potato plant, a squash plant, pumpkins and cucumbers - our "marine" gardens. Whoever got there first and saw the sprout come up would put a stick and it would automatically become his. You tended it all summer until you got your vegetable from that little bush. There might be five or six varieties of vegetables along the shore line. If you had more than you needed, your neighbor got his share and would swap vegetables with you from his claim.

This is my Dad, Gene Titus and me with fresh lobsters. The photograph was taken in 1929.

In the summer months along the shores, the herring (small sardines) used to come in close to the beach. Dad would cut the heads off them, degut them and put them in vinegar and soak them overnight, then fry them next morning for breakfast. Yum! We would put the herring in nail kegs and row out to the lobstermen and they would swap a lobster for a keg of herring. We also had our own lobster and crab traps and I can remember baiting my crab trap and leaving it two days instead of one. Then I couldn't pull it up. I had to row it ashore and empty it when the tide went down. That trap was full of great big rock crabs. We would go down to the pier and catch mackerel. Mom would salt them in a crock for a winter meal. We would row out to near Boston Light to get our codfish and flounder. Clams were plentiful off our beaches. Once my cousin, Elizabeth, was visiting and she decided she wanted to eat periwinkles. We went down to the beach, picked up periwinkles, found an old tin can around the house to put the periwinkles in, built a fire and cooked and ate them. Its a wonder we didn't have ptomaine poisoning.

During northeast storms the tide surge carried the water over the sea walls and flooded the interior of the island.

When the northeast storms would hit the coast they were really fierce at the northeast corner of our island. We had a seawall there that was built up out of great big granite slabs, two feet by four feet by six feet. On the outside there was just general stone dumped over them to protect the walls. When a northeast storm would come we used to go up on top of the hill by the gun emplacement and watch the waves break over and hit those stone walls. Sometimes, when the weather was warm and we didn't mind getting wet, we used to run down on to the stone wall, wait for a wave to hit and then try to outrun it. If you were lucky, you outran it. If you weren't, you got drenched. I've seen waves take those great big granite slabs and just tip them over like they were little blocks of wood. The waves were so powerful they would vibrate the house when the hit the seawall.

As I told you, the house was seven feet off the ground on a full cement foundation. You can see by the picture we had a large front porch that faced south. In the summer it was screened in and you could sit out there and watch the evening sun set over Boston. During the morning the east sun would come up and it would be a beautiful place to sit. In the winter, it was a little cold. Sometimes when the wind was northeast we would use the back door which was on the opposite end of the house. In the basement we had a cistern - a cement box built of bricks and cement and whitewashed - with a wooden cover on it. Although they used it to store water in the old days, as I remember we never kept water in it - we had fresh water brought in by a water pipe from Boston. When we lived there, the cistern was always empty and it was just a shelf to store things on. In the cellar there were set tubs in which we did our laundry and a big coal furnace. There was a cupboard where my mother stored her jars of preserved goodies. In bad weather, we played down there and my mother hung her clothes there in bad weather. Out the northside of the house, the bulkhead went up seven feet and down on the outside for seven feet.

The first floor consisted of a long hall off the front porch. On your right was a closet. On your left was the living room. In the picture, you can see the bay window in the living room. The living room in those days was used for special guests. If you went in to play the piano or phonograph, you had to be clean and you didn't bounce on the furniture. My mother had a beautiful seven foot runner on one of her ferns and it would travel all the way across the back of the divan. She used to trim it and I remember one day she came out into the kitchen with tears in her eyes - she had accidentally cut one of the longest runners of the fern so she had to start all over again. She had plants all over the place. I remember the big brass kettle she had with a big lion's head on each handle. That was for ferns and they draped to the floor. Further down the hall to the right were the stairs that went upstairs. A little further on was the cupboard where the brew was kept. Then you came into the kitchen. On your left was the stove, the hot water tank and on your right was the kitchen table and on the left was the door going into what was the dining room.

The dining room was actually filled with great huge bay windows that faced towards Boston. When Boston airport became bigger, the planes' headlights would shine right in our window when the planes were taking off. As you went across the kitchen to the far side on your left, there was a walk-in pantry. The icebox was in there. We never did have electricity other than the power plant that we tried to run that time. A boat delivered ice and you lugged a chunk of ice to the icebox. As you went straight ahead, you came to the back entry. The back entry was where you kept you daily clothes and the broom, mop, guns and it took you down to another catwalk which ran right alongside of the house from the front porch to the back and it angled over to the woodshed and then back by the house to the big tower, made a turn and headed east to the little tower and then to the oil house.

On the second floor of the house, on your left, was Mom and Dad's room on the end towards the porch so he could look out and see the towers. Each of the towers had a little square window on the backside so you could tell at night whether the light was burning properly or not. On the right side of the hall was my bedroom and straight on down the hall and on the right was the guest bedroom and straight at the end of the hall was the bathroom. We had an old fashioned bathtub with legs and the old toilet with a high tank and a large wash basin. We had hot water gravity heat and there were radiators in every room. There were storm windows and it was always very comfortable. There was painting to be done all the time on the lighthouse, winter and summer. Our water and telephone came from Boston underwater by pipe and cable.

Every once in a while they used to have to dredge the old army dock out because the sand and gravel built around it. When the dredge, *Bay State* used to come (about every two years), I was in my glory. I used to row out at lunch hour and eat with the crew on the dredge. It was quite an event to get out there and tie my skiff along side the beg dredge, then climb up on the dredge. After lunch, I would go up in the pilot house and watch them run the levers which walked the dredge along and watch the thing dig up the dirt and fill the barges that were alongside. In those days instead of suction they used a clam bucket and they would dig down into the water and bring up the dirt and put it in the barges. When the barges were full, they were towed off shore and dumped. These dredges would have cables running to the beach to stabilize them against the winds and tides. I also used to row out and wait for the cable to lay down when the dredges swung the bucket down to the bottom of the sea. The cables were slack so you would row like a son-of-a-gun to get over the top of them so that when they picked the bucket up and laid it over on the barge and tightened you wouldn't get hung up on it.

The mailboat came in at 8:00 a.m. so you would be off by seven to make your rounds in order to end up at the pier in about an hour. On the west side of the island it was all beach but on the east side it was granite rocks brought from Quincy quarries out on big barges and piled up to keep the seas from crashing through the island. They were jagged rocks, six, seven and eight feet in diameter. We would leap from rock to rock to see how fast we could run. I look back and wonder how I ever managed to do this without a serious fall and breaking a leg. We would look for relics that came up, like lobster traps, sometimes after a storm. If it was a lobster trap, we would find out who the owner was and take the trap back to him and they would give us a lobster or two as a reward.

As you came off the pier, there was what they called the engineer's office. The engineer corps kept their blueprints there when they were doing work in the harbor. It was also a meeting place in the winter months where people waited for the mailboat. Behind this office, cut into the back of the hills, there was a set of wooden stairs that went to the top of a high hill. Under the stairs there was a cave with thick, wooden doors and a tunnel. The tunnel was started to be dug from Lovell's Island to Fort Warren during the Civil War but was never completed. It came out on the beach and you could see the dome of it on the beach at low tide. We kids would play down there among piles of bundled newspapers and climb over them and try to spook each other. In a book by Edward Rowe Snow, THE ISLANDS OF BOSTON HARBOR, copyrighted 1971, on page 168 he tells about this tunnel but he had no answers for it either.

On the Army dock, thats Dad on the right, Sergeant Daley in the center and Edward Rowe Snow on the right. Mr. Snow brought Christmas packages to the five families on the island. This was before he was the flying Santa.

Chapter Fourteen

A fourteen day leave for Dad. Mom and our camping trips, surfing, the two holer and a little help.

This is what Provincetown looked like in the late 1920's. The post date on the back of the card is 1929. *Post card loaned by Stanley Snow, Orleans, Mass.*

Chapter Fourteen:

My Dad used to get leaves (vacations) in the summer as a rule. He would get fourteen day shore leaves and a substitute would come out; otherwise he would have to pay for a substitute to relieve him which I know he did once in a while. On those fourteen days, he used seven of the days in Maine and seven down in Provincetown. When we went to Maine with him, my Uncle Lawrence Gilmore, who lived Downeast in Hampden, Highland, treated me not as a city boy but had me doing the farming and haying, trying to milk cows and various other chores. So, I used to love to go up there.

Provincetown was Dad's hometown and we visited relatives and friends there. I can remember one house right across from the town hall - on the right hand side of the memorial (the Pilgrim Monument), when there was a full porch around it which had vines growing over the front of the porch. Back in those days, you had to sit and not be heard from. When the weather was bad, I would go inside where they had a cuckoo clock. I used to love to sit there waiting for that cuckoo to come out. They had a parrot. A very talkative parrot and in the summer months he was put out on the porch but no one could see him because of the vines. The porch was also screened in. I used to love to sit there and listen to him. Someone would come by and the parrot would yell, "hello, hello," and people would say "hello, how are you?" and the parrot would carry on a conversation with these people who would think it was someone sitting on the porch.

When I got older and into high school, there were times I couldn't go with him on vacations because the relief man came at the time the service designated. This might be school time. One school period break, I went home to the island when Mr. Rogers was substituting for my Dad. These men were all brought up with Dad in Provincetown - all local seaport people. They didn't reveal secrets about your parents very often but Mr. Rogers got talking to me and asked if my Dad had ever told me about the time when they were kids down on the Provincetown Pier. They were chewing tobacco to see how far they could spit it. "Your grandfather Jennings, was very strict against smoking and chewing. Your father and I had a mouthful of tobacco when your dad looked up and there was your grandfather behind him. Your grandfather asked 'how are you doing, son?' So Charlie (my Dad) swallowed and said, 'Fine, Dad.' When your grandfather left, your father upchucked." (I don't think he ever chewed again.) "Also, did you hear about the time he got caught smoking? We used to go out in the shed and smoke little stogie cigars which, after smoking on them a bit, we would nip off the ends and hide them up on the rafters, not realizing your grandfather could smell the smoke. One night, at supper, your grandfather said 'Well, Charles, I found a little something that belongs to you. I want you to light up and enjoy it.' He made your dad light up the old stogie and your dad puffed and puffed until he turned green. It was some time before your dad ever smoked again and then it was a pipe." When my dad came back from vacations, I related these tales to him. With a sheepish grin my dad said, "Wait until I see Rogers about giving away my secrets to my son".

My mother would take trips when dad wasn't on vacation and she would take us kids camping. One time, Jimmy Small and I came down to Cape Cod with our mothers. We had a 9 x 12 umbrella tent and a 1927 Buick touring car. As you can see in the picture, Mrs. Small, my mother, Jimmy and I camped right next to Highland Light. In those days you could pull off the dirt road, clean out a space and pitch a tent. No one objected. We frequently camped down by the old pumping station at the bottom of the hill in North Truro and pick blueberries and beach plums which ever was in season. My wife, Hattie and I used that same 9 x 12 tent when we got married on June 28, 1942.

These photographs were taken in Truro on Cape Cod on one of our vacations. In the top photo, taken at Highland Light, I am on the left and Jimmy Small is on the right. In the middle left photo, Me and Jimmy used to "water up the sands", with me on the left and Jimmy on the right. In the middle right photo, our 9 x 9 umbrella tent. Mrs. Small on the left, Jimmy in front of her, Mom on the right and me in front of Mom. In the bottom photo is a picture of the touring car. This was taken next to the North Truro pumping station.

111

When I was a boy, we did "dory surfing". We used to take the 18-foot dory, row it to the spit between Brewster Bar and Bugs Light at the south end of the island. When the tide was just right and the rollers would come in from the east, we would get the dory going over the breakers by walking back and forth inside of the dory to keep the dory balanced on top of the wave and ride it through the narrows for quite some way. Then we would row back again over the breakers and wait for another good wave. One of the boys would sit in the stern with an oar and steer (usually the youngest boy). This was "dory surfing" like they do today with boards.

Attached to the back part of the woodshed, we had an outhouse - a two holer. We had modern bathrooms, but if we were out playing, working or painting and were dirty, we had to use the outhouse. We couldn't go in the house. There were a lot of cobwebs there so you would have to remove the cobwebs before you could go because the outhouse wasn't used that often. In the cold weather it sure was drafty.

The service sent a special crew out to do things that Dad couldn't handle himself. A crew came out one time to do some shingling on the roof. Dad was on a salary and we had to eat off the salary but the house and fuel was given to my Dad free. This time he had to feed four more men without additional compensation. So, they had to eat what dad put on the table. These men all grew up with dad and would ask, "What are you making, Charles?" "Never mind, just eat it." He would have big pots of clam chowder and stews which were delicious even though you never knew what was in Dad's secret menus but the crew ate more than their share. Actually, when he could, Dad cooked our meals and Mom did the baking, except for doughnuts and jelly rolls. Every Saturday morning as far back as I could remember, Dad made doughnuts. When the mailboat arrived at the island at 8:00 on Saturday morning with its three man crew, Dad would have three little bags of doughnuts for each of them. Captain Jennings' doughnuts were a Saturday tradition. There was always a lovely table set at mealtime, although the wages were not that high - $840 a year in the beginning, less than $1,000 by the time my dad left the service. We lived good and during the Depression we lived a lot better than some of the other people in the area. During the Depression he took a $60 cut in pay for a while.

Chapter Fifteen

Harbor happenings, I can't swim, they are ruining our guns, it can scare you and I am at last a wickie.

The "J" boat *Rainbow* under full sail. A beautiful racing sailboat.

Chapter Fifteen:

Dad had a good knowledge of knots because as a lad he was a crew member on a two masted schooner out of Provincetown for one summer. The owner of the yacht allowed no cloth - everything had to be made out of canvas, rugs had to be made out of rope and doilies on the table were made out of canvas and ropes. Dad knew many quick ways to tie knots and I wish I had paid more attention.

Back in the 1930's, they raced what they called "J" boats in defense of the America's Cup. There was a racing sloop called the *Rainbow* that had an enormously high mast. I remember seeing her make the turn to come through the narrows which was rare for a boat of that size sailing. I ran down to the pier, hopped into my skiff and rowed out. As I got near her she sailed by me and there was a man up on the rigging at the top of the mast. With the boat laying over, he was directly over my head about 200 feet from my boat. I found out later he was up there so if anything went wrong with the rigging he could cut it loose. Things are done differently nowadays.

Another race that took place was between the Nova Scotian *Blue Nose* and the American fishing boat *Gertrude Theabeault*. These two boats were the last line of the old fishing schooners that sailed and fished. They raced these boats because they were the traditional fishing boats that fished on the grand banks and raced back with their catches. They were the same class of schooner. They had engines in them but they weren't used for this race. They raced off the Graves Light and one afternoon when an easterly breeze came in, a mirage took place. The boats were sailing in a light breeze and up in the sky you could see a reflection of the boats - a boat in the water and the same boat upside down in the sky, the tips of their masts joined.

My mother had been around the water all of her life - traveled back and forth in dories and power boats in all kinds of storms - but could not swim a stroke. She always said, "If I go overboard, I'll drown." I only saw my father swim once or twice. I didn't do much swimming - the water was too cold, although I had to learn enough to swim from the end of the pier to the beach before I could go out in a boat by myself. One warm day a man from the army - he had been in Panama for a few years - decided to go swimming. He put his bathing suit on, came down to the pier which was probably about fifty feet from the end of the pier to the beach. He dove off the end of the pier and when he hit the water he came up and skimmed across the top of the water without stopping, came out of the water, ran up on the beach and ran all the way home without turning back. When he came back fully dressed, he said he had been so cold he never caught his breath until he got to the barracks.

Back in the 1930's a disarmament treaty was made with the Germans to seal off the six inch disappearing guns behind the house on the island. Diplomats from several countries were there and we kids were warned not to go near them because of security reasons. But we had our secret paths up the back part of the hill that we used to watch the guns when they used to fire them. They had drilled large holes through the recoil barrel of the gun and put big pins in so they couldn't be used anymore. German dignitaries came over to make sure the guns were pinned down. We watched the whole scene from the bushes on top of the hill and weren't caught.

Fog can be hair-raising, deceiving and very scary. One time we rowed over to Gallop's Island and took the quarantine boat to Boston. Coming back, the fog was in. There was a boat called the *Eureka* of the Boston Sand and Gravel Company which towed two sand barges from down around the Marshfield area and came into Boston every weekday afternoon. The boat had a long cable between her and the barges and in the forward end of the *Eureka* there was one mast. She would blow her whistles - one for herself and one for each barge, one long and two shorts. We heard her coming but the Captain didn't blow often enough and we couldn't keep track of her. We were rowing from the island and Dad put me up in the bow of the dory and said, "Son, if you see anything, yell!" It was low tide and you couldn't see more than twenty feet ahead of you when all of a sudden this mast appeared. I screamed to my Dad and he backwatered with the oars. When we got ourselves oriented we found it was the pilings on the pier that we were headed for over on our island rather than a ship's mast. As I said, fog can be very deceiving and scary.

In April, 1939, Dad was taken sick with high blood pressure and kidney trouble. Mom had to tend the two lights and go up and down the two towers three times a day. At that time, I was a junior in high school in Hingham, Massachusetts. I quit in April because my Mother couldn't get a substitute for the light. I was eighteen years of age so I tended the light until my father took disability retirement on May 25, 1939. During those two months I was paid $55 a month. I was called a "wickie", which is what the lighthouse keepers were called in those days because the lights were lit by kerosene lamps and wicks. Dad and Mom moved to Maine, bought an old farm which had been abandoned and began restoring it. Our furniture had been loaded for the last time on the USLH's tender *Shrub* to be taken to the Chelsea depot and to a moving van for the trip to Searsmont, Maine. I repeated my junior year in Liberty High School in North Searsmont, Maine. Dad passed away March, 1940 about one year after his retirement. I stayed in school until the end of the school year and then I had to go to work to support my mother as Dad's retirement ended at the time of his death. Four or five years later (through legislation that was passed) Mom started to receive a widow's pension.

****

Thanks to the United States Lighthouse Society, 964 Cheney Street, San Francisco, California, 94131, the existing lighthouses of America will be preserved so young (and older) people may see what the life of a lighthouse keeper's family was like.

EPILOGUE

After my Dad passed away, I stayed in school until the spring break. With no income, I had to go to work to help support my Mother and myself. I worked on the Searsmont highway department helping to grade the many dirt roads. When the blueberries became ripe, I raked, packed and shipped. Next came the corn. This was September and the end of work.

We knew we had to move to where there was work. In the meantime, my uncle Chet Curtis, who worked in the Fore River Shipyard, called and said he had a job in the plumbing maintenance department. I took the job. It was now October, 1940. A few months later, Uncle Chet called and said I could transfer to the coppersmith department and start a training course. In the summer of 1941, I met Harriet Harper and on June 28, 1942, we were married.

In June of 1943, Uncle Sam pointed his finger at me and said "We need you." So I went in the Navy as a "coppersmith" until December 1945. I did my tour of duty aboard the repair ship *Argone, AG31.* I boarded the ship at the Solomon Islands in the South Pacific. We went up through the various island groups to the Philippines and then on to Tokyo, Japan.

After I arrived home, I went to work for Armstrong Cork Company of Braintree, Massachusetts, for five years. These five years were inside work and I was not happy. In May of 1951, a family friend introduced us to North Eastham on Cape Cod. Hattie, our son Charles (born 1948) and I bought two lots and started to build our home. I worked with a local plumber. In April, 1954, I started my own plumbing business. In February, 1984, I took part time retirement. Charles, our son, ran the business until June 20, 1988, when we sold the business. Now being fully retired, I completed the work on this book.

****